LIVING IN THE LAB

without smelling like a

CADAVER

LIVING IN THE LAB
without smelling like a
CADAVER

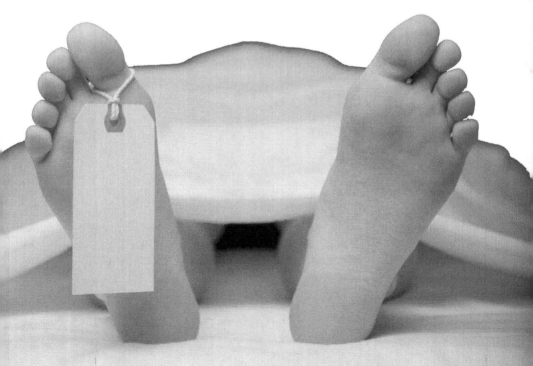

William C. Peel, ThM

The Paul Tournier Institute is the educational division of the Christian Medical & Dental Associations. The Paul Tournier Institute sponsors conferences and creates resource tools developed to help physicians, dentists, and other healthcare professionals investigate and discuss how the world of faith can be integrated with the world of biomedicine.

The Christian Medical & Dental Associations was founded in 1931 and currently serves more than 16,000 members; coordinates a network of Christian doctors for personal and professional growth; sponsors student ministries in medical and dental schools; conducts overseas healthcare projects for underserved populations; addresses policies on healthcare, medical ethics and bioethical and human rights issues; distributes educational and inspirational resources; provides missionary doctors with continuing education resources; and conducts international academic exchange programs. For more information:
Christian Medical & Dental Associations
P.O. Box 7500, Bristol, TN 37621-7500
888-230-2637
www.cmda.org • main@cmda.org

Table of Contents

To
Dr. Walt Larimore
who smells great even after living
in the lab for more than twenty years

Foreword
by Dr. David Stevens

"Beware: Entering Crisis Zone!"

That sign could aptly adorn the gateway to every medical and dental school campus today. Medicine and dentistry are changing at warp speed. The crisis is causing doctors to drastically change their perception and practice. And in some cases, the crisis is causing casualties.

Doctors are watching their ancient healing art transformed into a cold business. The time-honored covenantal relationship between doctor and patient is giving ground to an ethically questionable contractual relationship. In a profession committed to "do no harm", what was unthinkable thirty years ago is now being recast as "good." Doctors killing their patients at both ends of life is becoming an accepted practice. Add to this deadly mix a postmodern culture that distrusts science spending billions on alternative medicines, blindly embracing unsubstantiated claims of modern day snake oil salesman.

How can a Christian doctor not only survive but also effectively minister in this battle zone?

I believe the answer is *comprehensive basic training*. Soldiers don't last long without it, and neither will Christian doctors in the cultural and professional wars in which we daily engage. Without basic training, our forces will shrink as we take more and more casualties and attract fewer and fewer to join our ranks.

Though it is never too late, the prime time for training is during the first two years of medical or dental school. That is when future doctors are shaping the core beliefs and practices that will guide their careers.

This book launches a core curriculum series for students, residents and graduate doctors around the world. Its goal is to answer the question, "What must Christian doctors know to integrate their faith and their profession—and to pattern their lives and practice after the Great Physician?"

The question CMDA has been asking is, "What essential principles must Christian doctors learn and do to become all that God calls them to be?"

First, you need to have a real and growing relationship with Jesus Christ and knowledge of the Bible. Just as basic sciences form a firm foundation in your healthcare training, persistently practicing personal spiritual disciplines are essential for a vibrant Christian life. Without them, no doctor can maintain spiritual health or realize the full potential we enjoy in Christ.

Second, students and graduates must learn and be shown how we can integrate our faith and relationship with God into our daily practice.

Third, Christian doctors must understand and defend themselves against culture's attack on marriage and family.

CMDA is committed to discipling students and graduate doctors—teaching you how to appropriately share your faith, providing opportunities for personal growth, equipping you with tools for effective ministry, and representing you as the voice of Christian doctors.

That is why I'm excited about the first module of our basic training curriculum. With God's help, there will be many more modules added to this inaugural volume.

The life of Daniel has always been a challenge to me as a doctor. Though he worked in a different profession, his example will serve you well as you follow your God and His calling on yoour life. Bill Peel has done an excellent job of applying Daniel's example to the healthcare profession.

As you master this material, take heart. This is not just something else to learn or be tested on. This material will *change your life*, bring you true satisfaction in your profession, and help you to please God—who has called you to serve him through healthcare.

And you have an edge, because all of us at CMDA are praying for you and cheering you on. We want you to be part of the great army that will change the heart and face of healthcare!

Where Is Healthcare Heading?

In April of 1912, the *Titanic,* the largest ocean liner ever built, sailed from Southampton on her maiden voyage from England to New York City. Some 882 feet long, the new flagship of the White Star Line was the crowning achievement of ocean-going technology and the new standard of luxury and safety for those traveling between Europe and America. At last passengers could travel the treacherous ice fields of the North Atlantic without fear. Double-hull construction and sixteen watertight compartments virtually ensured that the ship was unsinkable.

But on April 14, shortly before midnight, the unthinkable happened. While steaming at high speed about sixteen hundred miles northeast of New York, the Titanic hit an iceberg in heavy fog, slashing a three-hundred-foot gash in her hull that flooded six of the "watertight" compartments. The ship sank into the icy depths of the North Atlantic in less than three hours. "In one of the 20th century's first major lessons on the limits of faith in technology, the ship proved tragically inadequate when it collided with reality."[1]

Two mistakes compounded the tragedy. First, the managers of the White Star Line were so confident of the ship's invulnerability that they failed to place sufficient lifeboats aboard for the

Please read thoughtfully and then answer the questions that follow in the "Time for Thought" section before your first meeting.

9

number of passengers and crew. Second, another vessel, the *Californian*, had stopped because of the fog and lay just twenty miles away from the sinking *Titanic*. Unfortunately, no one was at the *Californian*'s radio to pick up the distress call. By the time she did receive the message, it was too late to do anything except join in the rescue of the fortunate few who fit in the lifeboats. Of the 2,227 on board, 1,522 perished that night.

Many of us think of medicine as unsinkable. As the passengers and crew viewed the *Titanic*, so men and women in the healing professions tend to view the tradition of Hippocratic medicine: the thought of losing this force for good in society is almost unimaginable. Unfortunately, medicine has altered its course, sailed into the treacherous seas, and hit an iceberg. Today a number of "watertight compartments" of Hippocratic medicine are flooding rapidly.

Essential elements that have kept medicine afloat, such as the sanctity of human life, absolute commitment to the patient's welfare, and the commitment to "do no harm," are all taking in water fast. Medicine is listing to port and will sink unless something changes its present course.

I am only one; but still I am one. I cannot do everything, but still I can do something; I will not refuse to do the something I can do.
—Helen Keller

The Challenge to Medicine

That's where you come in. As a student, you are the future of this great institution. Never before has more been asked of you. Many medical specialties have been saddled with the task of unraveling some of our culture's knottiest ethical dilemmas: When does life begin? When does it end? When does life have or cease to have value? Should we manipulate its basic composition by genetic engineering? Even, should we create life? In the past these questions were answered by theologians and philosophers responding to absolute truth. Today they are in the hands of medical scientists walking through a swamp of relativistic thinking.

In addition, medicine is being sent the bill for society's biggest failures. According to Dr. Leroy Schwartz of Health Policy International, social problems have become healthcare problems—to the tune of $134 billion per year.[2] Our clinics and hospitals are filled with the evidence of our social chaos.

As society creates more and more disease, doctors are also being blamed for how fast costs have risen; they have been asked to cut costs and to distribute medical resources under a whole new set of values. These values often pit the doctor's self-interest against that of the patient, offering incentives for cost containment.

Medical Costs for Social Problems[3]
Alcohol Addiction—$50 billion
Drug Abuse—$6.4 billion
Sexually Transmitted Diseases—$19.4 billion

Does hope exist when abortion has become enshrined as a necessity of convenience and choice? When states consider the acceptability of physician-assisted suicide? When medicine has become in many places an economic enterprise rather than the moral endeavor it has been for twenty-five centuries? When "Can we?" has replaced "Should we?" as the only ethical consideration? Where greed and materialism dominate the ethics of men and women—men and women who once responded to a noble calling from God?

The Hope of Medicine

How this challenge to the heart of medicine turns out depends on one thing. That one thing is not who is in the White House or occupying the Surgeon General's office. The outcome won't be determined by the growth of managed care or corporations who broker medical services. The fate of medicine in America hangs on one thing—what happens to your heart over the next years of training. The character and moral integrity of individual doctors will determine the future of healthcare. God help us if you fail to develop your heart during your training.

> Never doubt that a small group of thoughtful, committed citizens can change the world. Indeed, it's the only thing that ever has.
> —Margaret Mead

Fortunately, there is hope. You may think that you are just a lowly student. You may say you and your peers are only a handful of individual healthcare practitioners, but as Chuck Colson says, "History pivots on the actions of individuals, both great and ordinary." In fact it was a handful of committed physicians under Hippocrates' leadership who wrestled medicine from the hands of an exploitative, greedy group of individuals some twenty-five hundred years ago.

As we will learn from a study of Daniel, a person of competence, character, commitment, and courage, one individual can make a tremendous difference in an entire culture. Even though Daniel wasn't a doctor, a study of Daniel's life can provide an excellent paradigm for you as a medical student.

We meet Daniel when he is first a student and then follow him through his long career in an environment that was anything but friendly to his faith. He faced a formidable academic curriculum that challenged him mentally, ethically, and spiritually. His very life was threatened due to the failure of colleagues during his internship. He served demanding and often unreasonable superiors. He was tempted to compromise his convictions to preserve his success and place of influence. He had to deal with the temptations of an affluent life-style and widespread fame. He faced the loss of his career because of an undeserved attack on his integrity from well-respected peers who were motivated by jealousy and contempt for his faith. On a daily basis he faced the burden of responsibility that not just one life, but thousands of lives depended on his skills.

Use the following questions to stimulate your thought.

GROUP LEADER: Discuss these questions in the group after you have read the beginning text aloud together.

If you would like to survive and flourish during experiences like these, then a study of Daniel's life can help you become the doctor God called you to be. Culture turns on the actions of individuals; again, Colson says: "We never know what minor act of hopeless courage, what word spoken in defense of truth, what unintended consequence might swing the balance and change the world." Such is the potential of any ordinary man or woman who desires to be faithful to God seven days a week, twenty-four hours a day.

TIME FOR THOUGHT

1. Think back over what you've read. What challenges have you faced already in medical school?

_____

_____

_____

_____

_____

_____

_____

2. What challenges to you see ahead?

◀ Personally _____

_____

◀ Ethically _____

_____

◀ Spiritually _____

_____

3. How will you face these challenges? _____

_____

_____

_____

_____

4. Read Daniel 1:1-6. Why was Daniel in Babylon? _____

_____

5. Why are you in medical school? _____

_____

_____

6. What evidence of God's sovereignty do you see in getting you where you are today? _____

_____

_____

_____

GETTING THE MOST OUT
OF THIS STUDY

This study was designed for a group of three to twelve people, to be completed in completed eight weeks, though it can be compacted or expanded according to the group's needs and desires. Each session has a content section followed by discussion questions. These questions are grouped in four daily sections so that if you choose, you can complete them in your quiet time in ten minutes per day.

Four Guidelines

As a participant you should be willing to agree to:

◄ Commit yourself to completing the assignments before the group meeting.

◄ Make the group meeting a nonnegotiable item in your schedule.

◄ Be an active participant in group discussion and prayer to the extent you personally feel comfortable.

◄ Pray personally for the members of the group.

Before you meet with :the group, think about whom you would like to pray for over the next few weeks.

The Benefits

If you want to survive and flourish as a doctor, this study is for you. You will learn:

◄ How to survive when the bottom drops out.

◄ How to find the safest shelter in the severest storm.

◄ How you can impact medicine beginning right where you are.

◄ How to seek divine guidance while in the trenches.

◄ How to develop a culture-changing faith.

◄ How to recognize opportunities in negative circumstances.

◄ How to maintain a relationship with God when everyone else is compromising.

◄ How to hold up under persecution and attack.

◄ How to appeal to authority for change.

◄ How to attract fellow students and professors to Christ without a pulpit.

◄ How to remain a man or woman of integrity and survive the test of success.

PRAYER PARTNERS

During the group, you'll need the prayer support of someone else. Use the following guidelines to set up your prayer teams.

1. Identify a group member whom you will pray for and who will pray for you.
2. Exchange requests. Keep it to one or two things for which you would really like God's help.
3. Find time to pray every day. If you have texting capabilities on your cell phone, exchange numbers and text the other person that you are praying for him or her.
4. Take a few minutes to update each other once a week.

My prayer partner is: _____

Address: _____

_____

Home Phone: _____

Cell Phone: _____

Notes

1. Robert D. Ballard, "Epilogue for the Titanic," *National Geographic Magazine*, 1987, vol. 172, no. 4, p. 459.
2. "America's social ills and our health care system: an interview with Dr. Leroy Schwartz," *Bulletin of the American College of Surgeons*, December 1994, vol. 79, no. 12, p. 21-5.
3. Ibid.

Living in the Lab without Smelling Like a Cadaver

One of the most memorable days in medical training is the first day of anatomy lab. One whiff of formalin will take most docs back to that infamous day. Many students I have talked to initially have a hard time eating after lab. It's not just the sights, but the smell. You raise your sandwich to your mouth and the scent from your hands makes you check to see what you are eating. After a couple of hours of intimate work with your cadaver, you start smelling like you're living in the lab yourself. And no amount of Dial soap will take away that awful aroma at the end of the day. You can't work in an anatomy lab and not pick up the odor.

Likewise, it's a rare person who can live and work in a morally dead environment without becoming personally contaminated. Character pollution seems to be one of the perils of living in a contaminated culture—even for Christians. Increasingly, the only difference between Christians and non-Christians is where they spend Sunday morning from 11:00 A.M. until noon.

On the other hand, many Christians have opted out of meaningful contact with our decaying culture, isolating themselves instead of striving to be a fragrant aroma of Christ to the world. You

DAY ONE: Read Daniel 1:6-30 and pages 17-24.

Gallup found that most Americans who profess Christianity don't act significantly different in their daily lives from non-Christians. In his words, those who attend church "are just as likely as the unchurched to engage in unethical behavior."[1]

17

know the type. All their friends are Christians. They fill every moment of spare time with fellowship with other Christians and Bible study. They look for a place to live surrounded by other Christians. They want to work only with Christian lab partners and study with other Christians. Their aim is to practice with other Christian doctors and have an all-Christian staff. Their only contacts with the non-Christian world are brief encounters that occur as they dart from one Christian group to another. Seemingly sensible, this kind of an attitude is actually deadly to the cause of Christ. Leighton Ford writes,

> This "closed corporation mentality," a sort of Christian isolationism, has been a constant barrier to evangelism. Many Christians have been so afraid of being contaminated by worldliness that they have avoided any social contacts with unconverted persons. As a result, they have no natural bridge for evangelism; what witnessing they do is usually artificial and forced rather than the spontaneous outgrowth of genuine friendship.[2]

If we follow Christ's example, however, we have no choice but to engage our culture and penetrate society. In doing so we will be called to mix with unbelievers and fraternize with sinners—to be alongside, not aloof from. Even a casual study of the Gospels reveals that Jesus went out of His way to cultivate relationships with worldly, sinful people. Sure, they ruined His reputation with the religious leaders, but they didn't ruin His character. He carefully walked the line between contact and contamination.

But this line is a difficult one. More than a few have been pulled into the current of the culture and have found themselves swept downstream

Living life in the holy huddle might prevent the message of Christ from being diluted, but it also prevents it from being delivered.

Christian isolation is a bizarre effort to cure the disease of sin by quarantining the doctors. With no patients to treat, the effectiveness of the cure is a moot point.

—Stephen Lawhead

before they were able to get an oar in the water.

Fortunately, when Daniel was thrown into the Babylonian current, he had well-developed spiritual muscles. He encountered numerous challenges to his faith and daily faced opportunities to compromise his commitment: some subtle, some overt; some calculated to subvert his faith, some seemingly innocent. Although submerged in a patently pagan society, Daniel was able to prosper spiritually. Like you, Daniel had no choice but to fully engage the culture of his day—a culture sometimes hostile to godliness. Despite this fact, he emitted a fragrant aroma of godliness. Daniel did not allow himself to be sucked into the cesspool of pagan culture. In three particular tests designed to destroy his faith, Daniel refused to compromise.

What About Bob?

Bob was a promising Christian internist who moved to town to set up his first practice. He was winsome, highly driven, and had a flourishing practice going in no time. Before long, however, his schedule began to show on his face and with his young family. He gradually withdrew from the other Christian doctors and stopped attending church. It wasn't long before rumors began to surface that he was having an affair with a nurse. When several godly doctors approached him, he rebuffed them and told them he was fine. A year later his world caved in; things got so bad that he turned himself in to the state medical association and checked himself into a rehabilitation program. But this was only after a great deal of damage had been done to his reputation as a doctor, to his family, and to the name of Christ.

I found out later that Bob had been offered amphetamines his first year in medical school. He had declined, but during review for his boards, he was desperate. He thought he'd do it just once. But once became every time he hit a crisis. Finally, it got out of hand.

Three Tests

A Test of Interruption

Life doesn't turn out the way most of us plan it. But few of us can imagine the severity of the sudden changes that interrupted Daniel's plans. Daniel was a young man who had everything going for him. One of the privileged elite of his day, he was intellectually superior—"quick to understand." He was a hardy physical specimen. On campus today Daniel would be a stud—a handsome, intelligent, winsome young man. Socially, Daniel was nobility, a relative of the king of Judah, raised with all of the privileges and status of royalty—wealth, power, and education. Incredibly, this life of position and perks did not give Daniel a fat head. He was not proud or arrogant. Neither was he soft and self-indulgent like many people with similar privileges. He was absolutely committed to God and refused to compromise himself in any area.

To sum it up, Daniel was a young man with a future. If ever there was a person who could say God owed him favor and blessing as a reward for being such a good guy, it was Daniel. Then his life was changed forever— his country fell to Nebuchadnezzar, King of Babylon. In one moment, Daniel's entire world was turned upside down. Taken captive,

> The man who has God for his treasure has all things in One. Many ordinary treasures may be denied him, or if he is allowed to have them, the enjoyment of them will be so tempered that they will never be necessary to his happiness. Or if he must see them go, one after one, he will scarcely feel a sense of loss, for having the Source of all things he has in One all satisfaction, all pleasure, all delight. Whatever he may lose he has actually lost nothing, for he now has it all in One, and he has it purely, legitimately and forever.
>
> —A.W. Tozer
> The Pursuit of God

he would never see his family or set foot in his homeland again. He would be taken to a land where his God was mocked. He would be required to serve an unreasonable tyrant who could take his life at the smallest provocation. He would suffer the pain and humiliation of castration and never be able to father children. Every dream a young Jewish boy could visualize evaporated under the Mesopotamian sun as Daniel and his fellow captives trudged eight hundred miles to their new home on the banks of the Euphrates River.

Rather than resist, complain, or give up, Daniel's response to this catastrophic interruption was to rest in the sovereign hands of God.

A Test of Fortitude

When the company of young Jewish hostages arrived in Babylon, their old life as Hebrews was over—they were Babylonians. To indicate this new authority and life-style, their new master gave them Babylonian names.

> ### What's in a Name?
> Daniel, "God is my judge," became Belteshazzar, "Bel's prince."
> Hananiah, "Yahweh is gracious," became Shadrach, "Command of Aku."
> Mishael, "Who is like God?" became Meshach, "Who is like Aku?"
> Azariah, "Yahweh has helped," became Abednego, "Servant of Nebo."

The Hebrew names that connected them with God were replaced with names that extolled three Babylonian gods: Bel, Nebo, and Aku. According to the young men's captors, Daniel and his friends now belonged to the victorious Babylonian gods.

Not only did Daniel have to endure this subtle brainwashing, he was to be thoroughly indoctrinated in Babylonian thinking by studying under the most learned scholars of Babylon. After that, he was to enter the King's service. His education was calculated to change the way he saw the world and to make him think like a Babylonian; replace his biblical perspective with a pagan worldview.

How did the young Jewish student respond to

this attempted indoctrination? He applied himself and mastered the curriculum. And he survived. He was so grounded in the truth of Scripture that the falsehoods did not master him. As immersed in the culture as he was, Daniel never let the culture penetrate him. He never forgot who he was or to whom he belonged.

A Test of Fidelity

Although Daniel endured his name change and participated in the educational system, there were some things that he knew he couldn't do. One was eating the King's food. The problem was not the lavishness of the food or the strength of the drink, nor was it the eating habits of a picky teenager. It was faithfulness to God. All the meat and wine in the King's household were first offered sacrificially to the Babylonian gods.

According to God's law, it would be idolatry for Daniel to partake. Since Daniel was an astute young man, he knew that Jewish idolatry was precisely the reason he was in Babylon. He refused to blur the line between right and wrong made clear in God's Word.

The way Daniel held to his beliefs in this conflict is instructive. *First*, it is important to note that *before* the situation presented itself, Daniel had made up his mind to be obedient to God, no matter what the cost. Verse 8 reads, "But Daniel *resolved* not to defile himself with the royal food and wine . . ." (italics mine). I've learned personally that making up my mind ahead of time is crucial to obedience. In the heat of the moment and the pressure of a decision, it's all too easy for me to rationalize. Taking time to plan ahead, when things are calm and I can think clearly through the issues, usually ensures that I will make the best decision. Otherwise it's easy for me to cave in to the pressure of friends or circumstance.

As for Daniel, the day he arrived in Babylon, his decision was already made. He would allow nothing to come between him and his God. Not even the preservation of his own life was worth sacrificing his devotion.

Second, Daniel had a cooperative attitude. The intention of the King's diet was not to undermine the young men's faith, but to preserve their health. Daniel took into account the motives of the official and planned his response accordingly. Something stands out about his conversation with the official: Daniel was both polite and respectful of authority. When asked to violate his conscience, he did not belligerently demand his rights or complain. Instead, he graciously asked permission to try another diet.

Third, Daniel offered a creative alternative to the problem. He recognized the dilemma: God strictly forbade idolatry, and the king held the official accountable for the good health of the young men. But what seemed to be an impasse was not a problem at all. Realizing these goals were not mutually exclusive, Daniel proposed a ten-day test of eating only vegetables (which were not offered to idols) to see if the captors' health would be as good as that of those on the regular diet. This plan allowed both the official and four young men to remain obedient—the official to King Nebuchadnezzar and the Jews to their God.

Fourth, Daniel waited on God for the results. Daniel had no way of knowing how the vegetarian diet would affect his physical condition in man's eyes. He did know, however, that it would affect the way he looked in God's eyes. As it happened, at the end of ten short days Daniel and his friends appeared healthier than the rest. God had honored their faith and obedience with such a radiance in their appearance that the King's official permanently changed their diet.

At the end of the time set by the king to bring them in, the chief official presented them to Nebuchadnezzar. The king talked with them, and he found none equal to Daniel, Hananiah, Mishael and Azariah; so they entered the King's service. In every matter of wisdom and understanding about which the king questioned them, he found them ten times better than all the magicians and enchanters in his whole kingdom. (Daniel 1:18- 20)

The Outcome

As a result of their commitment, we read: "To these four young men God gave knowledge and understanding of all kinds of literature and learning. And Daniel could understand visions and dreams of all kinds" (Daniel 1:17). God blessed the four young men not only with superior wisdom, but with spiritual insight as well. The key that unlocked the door of spiritual insight was their obedience.

It's hard to read about Daniel and not marvel at the distance he traveled from hostage to honor graduate. He not only survived the lab but came out smelling like a rose, because he knew his God and was committed to obeying His Word. Before Daniel enrolled in the graduate program in Babylon, he had received his undergraduate education in the Scriptures in Jerusalem. Therefore, he could say with David,

> Your commands make me wiser than my
>   enemies, for they are ever with me.
> I have more insight than all my
> teachers, for I meditate on your
>   statutes.
> I have more understanding than the
>   elders, for I obey your precepts.
>   (Psalm 119:98-100)

DAY TWO: Use the following questions to stimulate your thought.

GROUP LEADER: Discuss these questions in the group after you have read the beginning text aloud together.

TIME FOR THOUGHT

1. What's your experience? Do you agree with Gallup that most Americans who profess Christianity don't act significantly different in their daily lives from non-Christians? _____
_____
_____
_____

24

2. Have you seen Christians engaged in unethical behavior? What kinds? _____

_____

_____

_____

_____

_____

3. On the other end of the spectrum are the Christians who want to spend their time only with other Christians. Why is this tempting? _____

_____

_____

_____

_____

_____

4. Re-read Bob's Story on page 19. Have you known anyone who has gotten into similar trouble? _____

_____

_____

_____

Why do you think this happened to Bob? What could he have done to prevent it? _____

_____

_____

What are the biggest potential areas of compromise in your life? _____

_____

_____

5. Have you ever had your dreams interrupted? What would you do if you had to drop out of medical school?

❑ Go crazy
❑ Shoot myself

❑   Be angry at God/tell Him to take a hike
❑   Accept it as God's will and look for what
    He wants me to do next
❑   Other _____
    _____
    _____

6. Has your education ever been a threat to your
   faith? How? _____
   _____
   _____
   _____

7. Have you ever been tempted to compromise
   your faith to avoid trouble? What was the situation? _____
   _____
   _____
   _____
   _____
   _____
   _____

   Real safety is a matter of presence, not place.
   Read Psalm 23. Is David safer retreating to
   the quiet streams or being surrounded by his
   enemies? Where are you safest? _____
   _____
   _____
   _____

8. Look at the way Daniel handled the food crisis.
   See if you can break down his strategy into
   transferable steps you could take in a similar
   situation where you were called to violate your
   conscience. _____
   _____
   _____
   _____

_____

_____

_____

_____

_____

_____

_____

9. Read Philippians 2:14-16. How is this command reflected in Daniel's life? _____

_____

_____

_____

_____

10. Read Colossians 4:5-6. How was Daniel gracious to his captors? _____

_____

_____

_____

_____

Are there any situations you've had to handle with grace and tact? _____

_____

_____

_____

_____

_____

_____

11. What situations do you need to think through now, so that you can draw the line ahead of time beyond which you will not go? _____

_____

_____

_____

_____

_____

12. Read Ecclesiates 4:9-12 and Galatians 6:1-2. Why is it so dangerous to be a loner? _____

_____

_____

_____

Do you think it was important that Daniel and his friends stuck together? Why? _____

_____

_____

_____

13. How does Daniel's obedience seem to be relevant to the way God blessed his academic success? Read John 14:21. _____

_____

_____

_____

_____

14. Read 2 Corinthians 2:14. Who around you is smelling the aroma coming from your life? What are they smelling? Does it smell alive or dead? _____

_____

_____

_____

_____

_____

Notes

1. *National and International Religion Report*, May 20, 1991, vol. 5, no. 11.
2. Leighton Ford, *The Christian Persuaders* (New York: Harper & Row, 1966), 71-72.

Holding Life Together When All Hell Breaks Loose

Dr. Rudd was the kind of obstetrician everyone loved. He took time with his patients and built a well-respected practice. Susan was one of his loyal patients. Dr. Rudd had spent hours helping her through a traumatic miscarriage and then through a normal pregnancy. On her third pregnancy, however, there were complications. During a late-term prenatal visit, Dr. Rudd discovered Susan had case of genital condyloma. He discussed with Susan the possibility of the baby's being infected and shared the medical options. Sadly, after birth the baby did develop laryngeal condyloma and after several surgeries, her voice was abnormal. An unfortunate and erroneous comment by Susan's ENT—that a C-section might have prevented this condition—unfortunately prompted Susan to call an attorney.

> DAY ONE: Read Daniel 2:1-45 and pages 29-36.

> Be strong and take heart, all you who hope in the LORD.
> —Psalm 31:24

Even though there is no medical support for the ENT's claim, and even though Dr. Rudd had provided the best medical care available, the lawsuit hit him like a ton of bricks. He cared about this patient, had done everything right, and now he was being blamed for the outcome and sued for malpractice. The case was eventually dropped, but for eighteen months the emotional weight was an

> Let nothing disturb you, let nothing frighten you: everything passes away except God; God alone is sufficient.
> —St. Theresa

29

incredible burden to carry.

These kinds of experiences make cynics out of many Christian doctors. There's no way, however, to avoid these dark threads woven into the fabric of the practice of medicine. One thing every doctor must learn is that the world in its present condition is a battleground, not a playground. But cynicism doesn't have to be the outcome. Amazingly, the doctor who suffers the deepest wounds, and has the most to complain about, often develops the greatest degree of love for and confidence in God. When everyone else falls apart, his or her faith holds life together. Like the calm in the eye of a hurricane, he or she experiences a tranquility that comes from a steadfast assurance of God's presence and power in the midst of chaotic circumstances.

> A little faith will bring your soul to heaven; a great faith will bring heaven to your soul.
> —Charles Spurgeon

Daniel knew that kind of calm—even in the face of crisis. You'd think that after being ripped away from his home and country, bombarded with temptations and tests, isolated from all but a few faithful friends, then having stood up faithfully under relentless indoctrination, Daniel, if anybody, deserved a vacation from problems.

Both God and men were so pleased with Daniel's performance that the young compatriots entered the king's service and surpassed all expectations. Life was finally making sense again to Daniel. There seemed to be a reason for his sacrifices. He was to be God's man in the court of King Nebuchadnezzar. His future looked very promising. Then the king had a bad dream—and hell broke loose.

The opening verses of Daniel 2 inform us that King Nebuchadnezzar's dreams were not sweet ones—they were nightmares. Evidently, the king assembled his entire house staff and asked for help.

Unable to comply with the king's demands,

and after desperate negotiations under the threat of death, Nebuchadnezzar's advisors admitted defeat. Understand that these men were not buffoons. They were the most learned individuals of their day, the wisest of the wise. But when it came to reading the mind of God, the best minds in the world are useless. Finally, the enraged king ordered the execution of every advisor, veteran and intern alike, including Daniel and his friends.

The picture would be almost comical if the proposed ending were not so tragic. The most powerful monarch in the world and the most intellectually astute sages of the day were all going to pieces—at least until they met a young man who happened to know the God who knows all things, even the thoughts of men.

What would you have done in Daniel's situation? I'm embarrassed to confess this, but I think that I would have fallen apart at the seams like everyone else. "Look, God!" I would have been tempted to say, "You know the misery index has been pretty high down here. This is no picnic, to say the least. But did You hear me complain? No, I studied my tail off. I kept myself pure. So I thought that maybe, just maybe, You'd give me a break. But no! What do I get for obeying You? A visit from the death squad!"

In contrast, notice Daniel's response. He didn't cry "Unfair!" to either God or man. Daniel kept his cool and was calm enough to accurately evaluate the situation, ask pertinent questions, and quickly suggest an alternative plan. Realizing that God was in control, Daniel decided to stick his neck out and try to be part of the solution. Seneca the pagan philosopher said, "Only Christians and idiots are not afraid to die." Daniel was no idiot. But, he knew God held his life in His hands and had absolute confidence that God could reveal the King's dream—if He chose to do so.

And without faith it is impossible to please God, because anyone who comes to him must believe that he exists and that he rewards those who earnestly seek him.
—Hebrews 11:6

As a doctor, you'll need that kind of cool, not only when you're under personal attack, but when your patient struggles on the verge of death and no one seems to know what is going on, much less what to do. Where does this kind of unflappable confidence come from? Certainly good education and experience will help you know good medicine. But that will only take you so far. You had better know the God of medicine.

The Secret to Calm in a Crisis

Pain, especially traumatic pain, has a way of compelling us to focus on ourselves. When we hurt, emotionally or physically, nothing else matters. Our awareness of the world around us shrinks in direct proportion to the intensity of our discomfort. Perhaps, like me, you've cried out, "God, where are You?"

When we feel as if God has shut the door and cannot hear our cries, it's easy for our faith to take wing and for us to panic. So how do we hold onto God even when it seems as if He has let go of us? Where does the faith come from to keep knocking when the lights are out and it looks as if no one is home? What is the source of a faith that doesn't take flight in crisis, that doesn't buckle under pressure?

God is our refuge and strength,
an ever-present help in trouble.
Therefore we will not fear, though the earth give way
and the mountains fall into the heart of the sea,
though its waters roar and foam
and the mountains quake at their surging.
—Psalm 46:1-3

When C. S. Lewis lost his wife, he wrote:

Meanwhile, where is God? This is one of the most disquieting symptoms. When you are happy, so happy that you have no sense of needing Him, if you turn to Him then with praise, you will be welcomed with open arms. But go to Him when your need is desperate, when all other help is vain and what do you find? A door slammed in your face, and a sound of bolting and double bolting on the inside. After that— silence. You may as well turn away.
—A Grief Observed

The answer is clear in Daniel's case: he knew his God. Daniel knew his God was present with him, not left behind in Jerusalem. He knew God was absolutely sovereign—even under difficult circumstances. He knew that God and God alone was the source of wisdom and knowledge, and that He loves to reveal Himself to those who seek Him with a whole heart. Daniel knew that nothing was concealed from God's mind. In short, Daniel had every reason to be confident, not because of the circumstances, but because of the person he knew God to be. Consequently, Daniel could be totally realistic about the threat of death and remain calm and optimistic about the outcome at the same time.

Keeping Life Nailed Down

Frankly, it is difficult to be realistic about life and remain positive at the same time. Idealism inevitably leads to disillusionment. Realism usually leads to despair. It's possible, however, to be realistic and avoid cynicism or hopelessness. Daniel's example can help us maintain equilibrium and keep life nailed down when all hell breaks loose.

Accept the fact that life is out of your control. The fact is that the things that matter the most to us in life are the things we control the very least. One sage said it well, "Life is meant to bring us a succession of experiences to show us our need of Christ." Whether our faith holds up or folds up will largely depend on whether the object of our faith is capable of controlling what we can't. In my opinion we never see God more clearly than through the lens of pain. When the help the material world offers grows thin and transparent, we can begin to see the "substance" of God, unclouded by earthly distractions.

Develop your knowledge of God. A strong faith in God is not something we inherit. Neither is it something mystical that falls on some, eluding

Ten minutes spent in Christ's society every day, aye two minutes, will make the whole day different.
—Henry Drumand

33

the rest. Faith is something developed, cultivated, and learned by each believer. It begins with knowledge—sound knowledge—of the object of faith.

Perhaps the reason so many of us let temporal problems weigh upon us so heavily is that we don't really know God, and the god do we know is not large enough to handle the problems we face. The little "g" in *god* in the previous sentence is not a typo. When we think inferior thoughts of God, we are considering an image constructed in our minds, an inference that has no reality in fact. Most men and women know God by hearsay and not personal experience. That "god" of our imagination is not God at all and is never capable to dealing with life. No wonder we panic when calamity comes. If we worship the invention of our minds or anyone else's, we will feel hopelessly on our own when life gets out of hand. And that is all too often.

What comes into our minds when we think about God is the most important thing about us.

The history of mankind will probably show that no people has ever risen above its religion, and man's spiritual history will positively demonstrate that no religion has ever been greater than its idea of God. Worship is pure or base as the worshiper entertains high or low thoughts of God.

For this reason the gravest question before the church is always God himself, and the most portentous fact about any man is not what he at any given time may say or do, but what he in his deep heart conceives God to be like. We tend by some secret law of the soul to move toward our mental image of God.

—A. W. Tozer
Knowledge of the Holy

Take the risk of faith. The cost of faith is always a risk. No risk, no faith—it's that simple. Knowledge *about* God translates into faith *in* God only when we take a risk in the crucible of life.

The only way we can develop the confidence that what we believe about God is true is to try Him out. That's why God allows the world to feel the pain of estrangement from Him. That's why health fails and good doctors get sued. God is shouting to us, "The world cannot help you, but I can. Try Me out. Keep knocking, not because you can see

34

a light on, but because you know that I am home. 'Never will I leave you; never will I forsake you' (Hebrews 13:5). Keep working not because you feel strong, but because I am working in you both 'to will and to act according to [My] good purpose' (Philippians 2:13). Keep demonstrating love to those hardest to love even when you feel empty and rejected, because I am 'able to do immeasurably more than all [you] ask or imagine, according to [My] power that is at work within [you]' (Ephesians 3:20)."

The more we step out on what we believe to be true about God, the more natural that kind of response becomes. Every time we exercise faith, our faith becomes stronger. As we step out, we meet the God of reality in our circumstances and find Him to be everything we hope Him to be.

There is nothing magic or mystical about faith. Whether it's faith in a friend, a physician, or God, it all develops the same way:

> The man who comes to a right belief about God is relieved of ten thousand temporal problems, for he sees at once that these have to do with matters which, at most, cannot concern him very long.
> —A. W. Tozer

learning ▶ testing ▶ experiencing ▶ believing

Faith is a function of our knowledge of God and our willingness to act on what we know Him to be. The more we act on correct knowledge, the stronger our faith becomes.

Develop close relationships with other Christians. Every student and doctor needs a group of committed peers. God is the ultimate refuge, but there are times when He uses a more tangible place of safety—sort of a hope-and-strength satellite care unit on earth. This kind of relationship isn't achieved in a church service staring at the back of someone's head. It happens in a group of people who look each other in the eye and talk about the hard issues of faith and life.

When you read the accounts of Daniel's life,

> Carry each other's burdens, and in this way you will fulfill the law of Christ.
> —Galatians 6:2

it is obvious that he and his three friends had this kind of relationship. Through the hardships of captivity and servitude in Babylon, they had grown not only in their faith, but also in their relationship with one another. They were committed to stand together, giving each other the support any one might need.

There will be times when we don't have the faith to ask God for what we need, but someone in the group will. There will be times when we hold up others when their faith fails. That kind of commitment and closeness doesn't develop overnight. It grows from a commitment to one another other built on the conviction that we need each other desperately in both the painful and prosperous times of life. It is built on the belief that God has given us each other for this kind of encouragement.

TIME FOR THOUGHT

1. How do you think you would have responded in Daniel's situation?
   ❏ Anger at God   ❏ Retreat
   ❏ Anger at the king ❏ Despair
   ❏ Self-defense   ❏ Prayer
   ❏ Other _____

2. Have you ever been accused of something of which you were innocent? How did you respond? _____
_____
_____
_____

3. Do you know a doctor who has been sued for malpractice? How did it impact his or her Family? _____
_____
Practice? _____

Personal life? _____

_____

Friendships? _____

_____

Faith? _____

_____

Was the suit deserved? _____

_____

How did it turn out? _____

_____

_____

How do you think you will respond when you
are sued the first time? _____

_____

_____

_____

4. Re-read C. S. Lewis' description of his feelings
   when his wife died (p. 32). Have you ever felt
   like this? _____

_____

_____

Do you think this was reality or perception?

_____

_____

Why does it seem so real?

_____

_____

_____

5. How important is it to you to be "in control?"

_____

_____

_____

When have things seemed out of control? ___
_____
_____

Did God seem distant or near at this time?
Why? _____
_____

6. What do these verses tell us about knowing
   God?
   Jeremiah 9:23-24 _____
   _____

   John 1:18 _____
   _____

   John 14:21 _____
   _____

   Philippians 3:7-14 _____
   _____

DAY FOUR

7. Read Daniel 2:17. Whom can you call in a crisis
   who will pray with you? _____
   _____
   _____

8. Read Daniel 2:18. What was the basis of the
   young captors' appeal to God? _____
   _____
   _____

9. Read Daniel 2:19-23. Whom did Daniel know
   God to be? _____
   _____
   _____
   _____
   _____

10. Many Christians try to use God to solve their problems rather than trying to use their problems to find God. Have you ever been tempted to do this? _____

Which do you do more often: worship or try to use God? _____

_____

_____

Read James 4:1-10. What are some dangers of using God? _____

_____

_____

11. Read Isaiah 40:25-31. What can we possibly encounter that presents a significant challenge to the power, wisdom, or knowledge of our Creator? _____

_____

DAY FIVE

What are some things that you might encounter that this passage speaks to? _____

_____

_____

_____

_____

13. Read Matthew 18:19-20. All of us need all of the praying we can get, whether we are in a crisis or not. What does this verse reveal about the power of group prayer? _____

_____

_____

_____

_____

_____

_____

_____

Keeping Your Ethical Edge

The hit movie *Indecent Proposal* may have caused as many Americans to question their moral ethics as any church service has in last few years. The moral dilemma the movie proposed was: Would you, or would you permit your mate to, have sex with someone else—for the right price? In the movie, $1 million did the trick. Unfortunately, ethical dilemmas are not just movie plots. They play themselves out in the honored calling of medicine as well.

DAY ONE: Read Daniel 3 and pages 41-49.

In its seventy-fifth anniversary issue, *Medical Economics* magazine noted several doctors who crossed the line. Orthopedist John Nork admitted in court to maiming at least thirty surgical patients. For nine years he made a practice of "performing surgery and performing it badly," just for the cash.[1] Everyone gripes about reimbursement problems, but another doctor, cardiologist Richard Kones, did something about it. Stealing from Medicare, Medicaid, workmen's compensation, Social Security, and six insurance companies, Dr. Kones collected $1.3 million in bogus reimbursement claims before pleading guilty to first-degree larceny.[2]

Although men and women like these are the exceptions rather than the rule, the temptation to step across moral boundary lines is something every doctor must face. As America debates physician-assisted suicide, it's apparent that some doctors will kill for a lot less than this.

41

Facing Ethical Dilemmas

While these physicians were clearly criminals and were caught, there are plenty of other ethical situations unbounded by law or ethical consensus. In the past, the moral compass of Hippocratic tradition at least throttled unbridled desires in medicine. Now new doors are being opened daily. Relativistic thinking has corroded the moral anchor of medicine. In a day when medical science has stopped asking "Should we?" and in its place has substituted "Can we?" one can't afford to remain ethically naive. The fact is, it's legal to do the wrong thing in many situations. To say nothing of physician-assisted suicide, the current ethical quandaries in genetics alone demand that Christians take a hard look at how they will respond when huge amounts of money, major social pressures, and the natural demands of medical practice collide with their convictions.

> When principles that run against your deepest convictions begin to win the day, then battle is your calling, and peace has become sin; you must at the price of dearest peace, lay your convictions bare before friend and enemy, with all the fire of your faith.
> —Abraham Kuyper

Anticipating what's just ahead, some obstetricians are beginning to consider their malpractice exposure for refusing genetic engineering. Though it's legal, they find it morally objectionable. At some time or another, all doctors must ask themselves what they would do in a situation where there's something either to gain by violating their conscience or to lose by doing what they think is right.

Sad but true, when medical science is looking for answers, the church is stuttering. Once dominant in healthcare, the church has largely disengaged. And what's more tragic, many Christian physicians have run for cover or become morally camouflaged. Often in the doctors' lounge, it's hard to tell many Christian doctors from non-Christian. They tend to use the same inappropriate language, tell the same off-color jokes, entertain themselves with the same morally debase movies and TV, treat their coworkers with the same lack of dignity, love their families only when it's convenient, and make decisions based on the same ethic of greed. They tend to drive with the same ferociousness toward the same ends as non-Christians—power, position, and possessions. Increasingly, the only difference between a Christian and his or her non-Christian colleagues is where they go after rounds on Sunday morning.

> You cannot play with the animal in you without becoming wholly animal; play with falsehood without forfeiting your right to the truth; play with cruelty without losing your sensitivity of mind. He who wants to keep his garden tidy doesn't reserve a plot for weeds.
> —Dag Hammerskjöldt
> *Sketches*

The Price of Compromise

The fact is that unless you are personally prepared, you will cave in or compromise rather than pay the price for doing what is right. We often forget that though there is often much to gain through compromising our integrity, there is also a price to be paid. Drs. Nork and Kones found that out the hard way. But there's an even higher cost—a cost that a few righteous Babylonian officials refused to pay even if it bought them acceptance and the opportunity to continue in their influential positions.

Well established in their careers as Babylonian officials, Daniel's three friends, Shadrach, Meshach, and Abednego, were offered a simple choice: bow or burn. Caught in the web of global politics, they were called to choose between their commitment to God and their lives. They had so much to gain by doing what they knew was wrong. With no other options short of compromising their faith, they chose to be faithful to God and suffer

43

the consequences.

Chances are slim that your life will ever be on the line for following your convictions. But make no mistake about it, you could face malpractice suits, loss of income, and even loss of your medical license by refusing to participate in certain forms of medicine that have become legal and medically acceptable, yet are morally offensive to a follower of Christ.

There will always be a price to pay for making a choice between right and wrong. The account of Daniel's three friends provides a clear paradigm of integrity for those of us who want to stand for what is right. The situation unfolds in Daniel 3.

> To go against one's conscience is neither safe nor right. Here I stand. I cannot do otherwise.
> —Martin Luther

Standing some twenty feet higher than the Colossus at Rhodes, and composed of or at least covered in gold, the image Nebuchadnezzar built must have been awe inspiring. Gathering the people before the image was calculated to unite the empire and to show the King's awesome authority, power, and willingness to crush (or toast) any disloyalty. So when the officials gathered, they were commanded to fall down and worship the image of gold when they heard the music play. It was a pledge of allegiance to Nebuchadnezzar and to the Babylonian gods.

Compare the image described in Daniel 2 with the one in Daniel 3. Any idea why the king made this image entirely of gold?

As thousands of the most powerful men of the earth bowed low to worship Nebuchadnezzar and his gods, three stood tall and worshiped the true King of kings. Noting the Jews' refusal to bow, the jealous Babylonians wasted no time in accusing the three Hebrews of treason.

Nebuchadnezzar's immediate response was not altogether unexpected. He was furious! But comparing the charges with the loyalty the men had exhibited over the years, Nebuchadnezzar offered them a conciliatory second chance. But it was a second chance with a warning—and a challenge to God.

Three Men—No Maybe

As for Shadrach, Meschach, and Abednego, they had to ask themselves some tough questions. What do we do in a situation that calls us to violate our conscience? How should we respond when there is a clear attack on our faith? How far can we go when asked to participate in something we consider evil?

These three men provide us with an excellent example to follow.

First, they knew where the line between right and wrong was drawn. They had no doubt that some things clearly violated God's law no matter where the men were or what the situation was. There was no last-minute debate. It was obvious to them how a godly person should respond.

They were honest about what they'd done. No slippery words with obtuse meaning were used to deflect guilt. They simply would not bow the knee to this image or any pagan deities. This was a black-and-white issue—no gray zones to discuss.

One of Satan's best tactics is to keep us talking and wear down our resolve. An old Russian fable makes the point quite clear. It seems a hunter came to a clearing. There stood a bear! When the hunter raised his weapon the bear shouted, "Wait! What do you want?" The hunter replied, "A fur coat." "That's reasonable," answered the bear. "I want a full stomach. Let's sit down and talk about it." So they sat down. After a while the bear walked away alone—he had his full stomach and the hunter had his fur coat. I'm sad to say there have been many times that I have stopped to discuss the matter and been eaten alive by temptation. I should have just said, "No!"

They refused to defend themselves. Shadrach, Meschach, and Abednego knew that this conflict was not about them. It was between two claimants for sovereignty over their

If you are ready to fall down and worship the image I made, very good. But if you do not worship it, you will be thrown immediately into a blazing furnace. Then what god will be able to rescue you from my hand?
—Daniel 3:15

45

lives. By getting out of the way, they made this issue very clear, which resulted in Nebuchadnezzar's challenge to God.

They affirmed their faith in God's ability to deliver. The reckless abandon these three men had with Nebuchadnezzar is astounding. But it was built squarely on their confidence in God. It is dangerous for anyone to try to read the future through the envelope, but God's power is always available generously giving His children the strength they need to face difficult circumstances.

They affirmed their complete submission to God and refused to obey the king. There was no name-calling, no antagonism—not even bitter words. They simply affirmed their allegiance to the God whom they believed ruled over Nebuchadnezzar. Then they believed that it was God's responsibility to call Nebuchadnezzar into account for the authority delegated to him as the king of Babylon.

Given the situation and Nebuchadnezzar's grandiose self-estimation, his furious response is no surprise. Yet as the king peered into the furnace, thinking he would see charcoal, his worse fears as a rebel and greatest hopes as a man merged. There was indeed a God who was able to rescue them from his hand!

Facing the Heat

Though you probably won't face fire, all Christians encounter situations where they must choose whom they will follow. If we want to follow God and honor Him like Shadrach, Meschach, and Abednego, we would do well to follow their example.

Prepare yourself mentally. If we don't want to get blindsided, we need to spend some time acquainting ourselves with the issues. Think ahead. What are the ethical minefields in your path as a student, resident, physician? What wisdom does the Bible give? What wisdom can you gain from others?

Prepare your heart before the test. It's not enough to know the right answers. In any circumstance we enter, we have a polarity—a predisposition based on whom and what we've been focusing on. Make no mistake about it. When there is an important decision to made, two worldviews will be at odds, both promising reward, and both guaranteeing a high cost.

Count the cost. Both compromise and integrity always have a price. Inherent in every decision are things to gain and things to lose, depending on the way we choose. Take our three Hebrew friends on the hot seat. Choosing integrity as they did could have easily cost them their lives. On the other hand, choosing to compromise would have cost them something far dearer.

Although nothing we do can separate us from God's love, every time we compromise, we damage the *intimacy* with our Father that channels His love to us. His attitude toward us never changes, but ours does—with ruinous results. Even though we remain God's children, when we compromise, we choose to live outside the tent of God's blessing.

Compromise costs us *self-respect* and others' respect as well. Far from gaining us approval, poor choices usually diminish our reputation.

You might want to get a copy of *Standards for Life*, a collection of the ethical statements of CMDA. Call 888-230-2637.

No healthy saint ever chooses suffering; he chooses God's will, as Jesus did, whether it means suffering or not.
—Oswald Chambers

LORD, who may dwell in your sanctuary? . . . He whose walk is blameless and who does what is righteous, who speaks truth from his heart.
—Psalm 15:1-2

Better is the poor who walks in integrity, than he who is crooked though he be rich.
—Proverbs 28:6
NASB

If I have to do the
wrong thing to
stay on the team,
I am on the wrong
team.

Compromise always *dishonors God.* No matter what your motive, the price of compromise is always loss of positive influence for God. Whatever we may gain cannot outweigh this tremendous damage. When we choose to remain obedient to God, we glorify God.

Put your welfare in God's hands. One of the greatest decisions every one of us makes is who will take care of us. Repeatedly God challenges His children to entrust themselves to His care. Any alternative will invariably lead us away from obedience. If I assume ultimate responsibility for my welfare, without fail I can expect to be offered a way to save my skin that will violate God's law. If I doubt God's protection, I will cut and run every time.

Find some other people to stand with you. God does not intend for us to stand alone. We need each other. This is especially true in the area of ethical decisions. Paul said, "Carry each other's burdens" (Galatians 6:2). I need other people with whom I can discuss the dilemmas of my life, who will encourage me to do what is right. I need others to stand with me shoulder to shoulder when I have to make a tough decision. And I need individuals who will lift me up when doing what is right costs me dearly. Integrity may mean standing alone, but it is enormously easier with confederates standing together.

After studying an extensive study of men in combat Colonel S. L. A. Marshal concluded, "I hold it to be one of the simplest truths of war that the thing which enables an infantry soldier to keep going with his weapons is the near presence of the presumed presence of a comrade. . . . It is that way with any fighting man. He is sustained by his fellows primarily and by his weapons secondarily. Having to make a choice in the face of the enemy, he would rather be unarmed and with comrades around him than altogether alone, though possessing the most perfect of quick-firing weapon."
 —*Men Against Fire*

Which system will you choose to live by? The controlling factor behind your choices is your knowledge of God. Is your knowledge of God strong enough to do battle with the doubts that will bombard your mind when you decide to step out and live distinctively for Christ?

Consider starting a student chapter of CMDA. For more information, call 888-230-2637.

TIME FOR THOUGHT

1. How do you think you would have responded in this situation?
   - ❑ Refused to bow
   - ❑ Called in sick that day
   - ❑ Bowed, but stood in my heart
   - ❑ Sat on the back row
   - ❑ Sat on the front row
   - ❑ Other _____

DAY TWO: Use the following questions to stimulate your thought.

GROUP LEADER: Discuss these questions in the group after you have read the beginning text aloud together.

2. Have you ever been in a situation like this? What did you do? What was the outcome?

   _____
   _____
   _____

3. What is the greatest challenge to your integrity today? _____

   _____
   _____

4. What ethical dilemmas lay ahead in your training? _____

   _____
   _____
   _____

5. What are the biggest ethical dilemmas today that medicine is facing? _____

   _____
   _____

_____
_____

What do you need to face these successfully?

_____
_____
_____
_____

6. Read 1 Corinthians 10:13. What is promised in this verse? _____

_____
_____
_____

Do you think most Christians believe this? How would we act if we did? _____

_____
_____
_____

7. Do a cost/benefit analysis of compromising your faith from the following verses.

Proverbs 11:3 _____

_____
_____

Psalm 16:4 _____

_____
_____

Romans 12:1-2 _____

_____
_____

Titus 2:9- 10 _____

_____
_____

Psalm 15:1- 2 _____
_____
_____

Proverbs 28:6 _____
_____
_____

8. Think about Shadrach, Meschach, and Abednego's decision to refuse to bow before the
image. Consider the following rational alterna-
tives. The obvious benefit is that they would
save their lives. But what problems do you see
with these lines of reasoning?

Rationalization: What good am I to God if I
lose this place of influence? I want to continue
to serve Him here in this strategic position.
Problems: _____
_____

Rationalization: The government (chief,
HMO) made me do it. I was just following
orders.
Problems: _____
_____

Rationalization: This will happen just one
time. I'm not making a life-styles of it.
Problems: _____
_____

Rationalization: God is gracious. He will
forgive me this once.
Problems: _____
_____

Rationalization: I don't deserve this. If God
can't take care of me, I have to take care of

myself.
Problems: _____
_____

Rationalization: It's a different world. We're a thousand miles from home, in a strange land, with strange customs. We don't want to offend our hosts. Besides, who will know?
Problems: _____
_____

Have you ever heard men and women in medicine use these same rationalizations for doing what they know is wrong? What was the situation? _____
_____
_____

What was the outcome? _____
_____
_____

9. When we rationalize unethical or immoral be-havior, what are we really saying?
   ❏ God doesn't care about some areas of life.
   ❏ God can't take care of me.
   ❏ I have to take care of myself.
   ❏ God doesn't want me to throw my life away.
   ❏ God helps those who help themselves.
   ❏ My agenda is more important than God's.
   ❏ Other _____
   _____

10. Read Proverbs: 17:17. Why do you think the Bible says so much about living in relationships with one another? Is your training thus far help-ing or hindering this need? What challenges to relationship and mutual support do you see ahead? _____

_____
_____
_____
_____
_____
_____
_____

Who will stand with you when the heat is on?

_____
_____

Notes

1. "Tales from the Dark Side of Medicine," *Medical Economics*, November 1998, p. 28-29.
2. Ibid.

Surviving the Test of Prosperity

If you're looking for the record number of malpractice claims, plastic surgeon Richard Dombroff could well hold the dishonor at 212. In the late eighties, he built a mini-empire based on the concept of same-day cosmetic surgery at his Personal Best center in Manhattan. At its peak, Dombroff's practice performed five thousand operations a year, generating a gross profit of about $5 million. His assembly-line approach to nose jobs, tummy tucks, and breast implants made Dombroff a rich man—temporarily—but at the expense of his patients. Eventually, Dombroff pleaded guilty to fraud for billing for reconstructive rather than cosmetic surgery and all but one of the malpractice claims had to be settled in a bankruptcy court.[1]

Though Dr. Dombroff is certainly an extreme, most doctors I know struggle with prosperity in some way. What is it that makes America's best-paid professionals wrestle with greed? Frankly, there is money to be made in medicine, even with the changes in healthcare. Very few doctors choose their profession primarily because of the financial opportunities. But by the time you enter practice, not a few of your colleagues—even Christians—will suffer from an odd malady. They will think they deserve a *very* comfortable lifestyle. After years of deprivation during training, it's not uncommon for the doctor and his or her family to

DAY ONE: Read Daniel 4 and pages 55-63.

Where your treasure is, there your heart will be also.
—Matthew 6:21

buy into the McDonald's jingle, "You deserve a break today."

The financial rewards that come to most doctors put them in an unexpected dilemma: how to survive success. You might think this odd, but there is something about success that tends to promote prideful self-sufficiency rather than a humble gratitude to God. Prosperity and spirituality have rarely gone together in human history. To make us truly wealthy, however, a very patient God at times depletes earthly wealth and thins our success. He ruthlessly and persistently pursues us to give us His very best. If we fail to honor Him in our prosperity, He graciously erodes our standing in the world until all we have to lean on is Him.

Losing it all can have a shattering effect on people. On the other hand, it can also bring us face-to-face with our utter dependence on God— and all the wealth we have in Him. Both of these were true of King Nebuchadnezzar. It is obvious that something dramatic has happened when we come to chapter 4 of Daniel's book. The entire chapter is the exact record of an official edict sent throughout the Babylonian kingdom.

Nebuchadnezzar himself wrote these opening lines, as well as the story to follow, to inform his kingdom of his complete submission to the one true God. His pilgrimage of faith included tests of both adversity and prosperity.

The Crisis of Success

Toward the end of his reign, between 586 and 562 B.C., with his enemies subdued and his grand building projects completed, the king tells us,

> Adversity is sometimes hard on a man; but for every one man that can stand prosperity, there are a hundred men that will stand adversity.
>
> —Thomas Carlysle

> Therefore I tell you, do not worry about your life, what you will eat or what you will drink; or about your body, what you will wear. Is life not more important than food, and the body more important than clothes?
> —Matthew 6:25

"I, Nebuchadnezzar, was at home in my palace, contented and prosperous." Unfortunately, even in the case of the wealthiest man in the ancient Near East, contentment with worldly prosperity was short-lived. Our gracious God would not allow Nebuchadnezzar or any of His children to be content with the meager wealth of the world. He made us for a richer existence, and deep inside our beings we know it. Whether God personally interrupts us, as He did with Nebuchadnezzar, or our spirit simply grows lean feeding on the empty diet the world provides, we soon learn that this world can't satisfy us.

> Prosperity knits a man to the world. He feels that he is "finding his place in it," while really it is finding its place in him.
> —C. S. Lewis

So God stepped into Nebuchadnezzar's path and filled him with disturbing images and visions. Finally Nebuchadnezzar called Daniel. Apparently, although Nebuchadnezzar disagreed with Daniel about religion, he nonetheless respected the Hebrew highly and trusted his integrity and competence. On hearing the King's vision, the Bible tells us that Daniel was "greatly perplexed for a time." It was not confusion that tied his mind in knots; it was concern. Daniel was alarmed. After close to forty years of serving this king, as different as they were, these two men obviously cared for each other.

> What good is it for a man to gain the whole world, yet forfeit his soul?
> —Mark 8:36

As any friend would do, Daniel appealed to the king to mend his ways. Note Daniel's compassion as well as his courage. It's doubtful any other man spoke this directly to Nebuchadnezzar and lived to tell about it. Courage is often driven by conviction—in this case it was also fueled by compassion. Daniel was so concerned, he put aside his own self-interest and moved to the aid of his friend. That's what love does.

This appeal didn't take place in a vacuum.

Lengthy conversations about sin, good and evil, and pleasing God must have transpired between Nebuchadnezzar and Daniel long before this crisis. Otherwise, Daniel's advice would have been meaningless to the king. Nebuchadnezzar knew the demands of a holy God. Unfortunately, knowing is not obeying.

How did the king respond? Perhaps he straightened up for a while, but soon his arrogance returned. He was hell-bent on doing as he pleased—dream or no dream. He was the most powerful man in the world. God was patient, but after twelve months the hammer fell.

With a swiftness that staggers the imagination, the mighty monarch became a raving maniac, racing from the palace, casting off his clothes as he ran. For seven unimaginable years Nebuchadnezzar lived and behaved like a beast on the palace grounds.

Nebuchadnezzar's state is no arbitrary condition, however. The essence of God's justice is always to allow us to feel the true implications of our choices. God had given Nebuchadnezzar the choice to live as a true human being, dwelling under the lordship of God's sovereign rule. By choosing to ignore his Maker, the king had reduced himself to the level of an unthinking animal.

Then God let Nebuchadnezzar taste the consequence of his choice. C. S. Lewis calls this way of judgment God's "kind hardness" or a "severe mercy." God is committed to interrupting the destructive behavior of those He loves, even if it means hurting them temporarily.

When Nebuchadnezzar woke from this

Appealing to Those in Authority

▼ Win the respect of authority.
▼ Develop a deep concern for his/ her welfare.
▼ Speak graciously.
▼ Outline the behavior to avoid.
▼ Outline the behavior to embrace.
▼ Outline the consequences of each.
▼ Be willing to stand by him/her whatever happens.

"This is what is decreed for you King Nebuchadnezzar: Your royal authority has been taken from you. You will be driven away from people and will live with the wild animals; you will eat grass like cattle. Seven times [years] will pass by for you until you acknowledge that the Most High is sovereign over the kingdoms of men and gives them to anyone he wishes." Immediately, what had been said about Nebuchadnezzar was fulfilled.
—Daniel 4:31-33

beastly living nightmare, it's interesting to note that he held no bitterness over his condition or the lost years of his life. On the contrary, he was absolutely grateful for the merciful interruption of his arrogance: "At the end of that time, I, Nebuchadnezzar, raised my eyes toward heaven and my sanity was restored. Then I praised the Most High; I honored and glorified him who lives forever" (Daniel 4:34).

> We talk of wild animals, but man is the only wild animal. It is man that has broken out. All other animals are tame animals, following the rugged respectability of the tribe or type. Man is wild because he alone, on this speck of rock called earth, stands up to God, shakes his fist, and says, "I do what I want to do because I want to do it, and God had better leave me alone."
> —G. K. Chesterton

Notice Nebuchadnezzar's eyes were no longer on "me and my" but on "He and His."

Passing the Test

In his epic novel *Ben Hur*, Lew Wallace wrote, "No person is ever on trial so much as at the moment of excessive good fortune." No doubt about it, prosperity is a much harder test to pass than adversity.

It's not a surprise to most of us who have reached our fortieth year that success is not only hard to enjoy, it can be downright hazardous to your health. One retiree echoed the sentiments of far too many when he wrote, "I let my job eat out the center of my life, leaving me only the crusts." Physically, reaching for the gold ring can destroy our health. Relationally, it seems much easier for greed and selfishness to take hold and drive us apart from those we love. Most damaging of all, however, is the effect that success and prosperity can have on our relationship with God. If God should bless you with success, what can you do to

> His dominion is an eternal dominion; his kingdom endures from generation to generation. All the peoples of the earth are regarded as nothing. He does as he pleases with the powers of heaven and the peoples of the earth. No one can hold back his hand or say to him: "What have you done?"
> —Daniel 4:34-35

59

make sure you pass the test? We can learn several things from Daniel and Nebuchadnezzar.

Acknowledge the source of prosperity. In Nebuchadnezzar's dream God made the source of the King's prosperity very clear. He called on Nebuchadnezzar to "acknowledge that the Most High is sovereign over the kingdoms of men and gives them to anyone he wishes." This idea runs totally counter to what most doctors think. If you asked a hundred successful doctors the source of their prosperity, you would hear answers like hard work, superior intellect, innate skill, or some other personal characteristic. You might even run into a Christian who believes success is a result of his or her obedience to God's laws. All of these reasons, however, place the source of prosperity in the wrong place—on man's shoulders.

It's clear from Scripture that God is the source of prosperity. He alone determines the boundaries of our lifestyle. While God will not allow us to claim total credit for gaining success, we can, however, cause the loss of success by our lack of faithfulness. On the other hand, don't make the mistake of thinking that the loss of wealth is necessarily a result of unfaithfulness. Take Job, for example. God said Job was absolutely righteous, yet he lost everything. In other words, my hard work, obedience, and sacrifice don't ensure my success, but the lack of these may very well precipitate my loss or lack of success.

Use wealth properly. If prosperity is a gift of God, it comes with an obligation to use it according to God's will. First Timothy 6 gives us some helpful insights into a biblical paradigm of success. Listen to Paul's instructions to the prosperous. Some very clear elements of the biblical paradigm of wealth emerge.

First, arrogance has no place in the life God has blessed with prosperity. To use the clothes I am able to wear, the car I am able to drive, the toys I am able to accumulate, and the house I am able to buy as a measuring stick, as an indication of my superiority, is an affront to God. If it is a gift, then I didn't earn it, deserve it, or acquire it on my own. So what have I got to brag about? It doesn't say a thing about my worth as a person. Far from making us proud, prosperity should make us extremely humble and engender a gracious toward others.

Second, we can't depend on prosperity as a source of security. Pearl Bailey is credited with saying, "Money isn't everything, but it sure does quieten my nerves." Granted, it might temporarily soothe our insecurity, but by its very nature it is "so uncertain," as Paul says. Those of us living in the at the edge of the new millennium know this to be true. Something so uncertain can't keep the hounds of insecurity at bay for very long.

Third, we can enjoy prosperity. God's unchanging intention is that we take pleasure from the gifts He has given us. We shouldn't feel arrogant about prosperity, but neither should we feel guilty about enjoying the good gifts of God. In my experience, only the person who hopes in Christ and understands that prosperity is a gift can really enjoy what God has given. When we rest our security on our wealth, we will always become entangled in preserving it—something we simply can't guarantee. When God says it's over, no man's grip is firm enough to hold it. Most people who strive after wealth eventually find that it controls them rather than their controlling it. When we know that Christ and what He provides is enough,

> Command those who are rich in this present world not to be arrogant nor to put their hope in wealth, which is so uncertain, but to put their hope in God, who richly provides us with everything for our enjoyment. Command them to do good, to be rich in good deeds, and to be generous and willing to share. In this way they will lay up treasure for themselves as a firm foundation for the coming age, so that they may take hold of life that is truly life.
> —1 Timothy 6:17-19

> There are two tragedies in life. One is to lose your heart's desire, and the other is to gain it.
> —George Bernard Shaw
>
> Few rich men own their own property. The property owns them.
> —Robert G. Ingersoll

then we can enjoy what God has given.

Fourth, we are to put our wealth to work. The attitude that prevents the enjoyment of God's blessings from slipping into selfish indulgence is compassion toward the needs in the world around us. Paul tells us we are to be "rich in good deeds, and to be generous and willing to share." In other words, we are not to use wealth as a security blanket or a score card, but rather as a tool. Whatever gifts God gives you, He intends for you to give away.

Putting wealth to work is something you need to begin to do today. Don't wait. Often students put this off, thinking that they will have more time, money, and resources to give later. But the sad fact is that if you don't begin now, it is highly unlikely you will change your giving patterns later. Take time now to give yourself away. Find a worthy cause to invest your money in—even if it's only a few dollars. Find someone to serve who cannot return the favor. Students have often found their greatest joy in serving in a clinic or a summer medical institute in the inner city. Whatever it is, don't wait. It may never get easier.

Understand prosperity's dangers. The fact that prosperity is so dangerous has made some Christians mistakenly run the other way, claiming poverty as a virtue. The fact is, vows of poverty

> Then I realized that it is good and proper for a man to eat and drink, and to find satisfaction in his toilsome labor under the sun during the few days of life God has given him—for this is his lot. Moreover, when God gives any man wealth and possessions, and enables him to enjoy them, to accept his lot and be happy in his work—this is a gift of God.
> —Ecclesiastes 5:18-19

Studies tell us that one percent of the nation's households own one-third of the nation's private wealth, sixty percent of the corporate stock, thirty percent of interest-bearing assets, and nearly ten percent of its real estate. Interestingly, the Bible never has a problem with the concentration of wealth to one group. God does, however, have a problem with the fact that this group statistically uses such a small portion of its wealth in any form of charitable causes. Interestingly, American households with incomes of less than $10,000 gave an average of 5.5 percent to charity, while those making more than $100,000 gave only 2.9 percent. I don't think that I would commend the latter group for being "rich in good deeds."[2]

are just as worldly as greedy ambitions—both focus on the externals rather than the heart. Every Christian needs to understand that if God has given or does give you prosperity in the future, it is a test as well as a blessing. Each of us needs to be aware of the personal dangers and watch for any sign of their infestation in our heart.

Make ourselves accountable to others. One of the greatest mistakes Christians make is to isolate themselves and their actions from the scrutiny of others. Accountability is important. It is difficult for me to spot the creeping pride, the intrusive superiority, the initial withering of the soul that can so easily occur as my eyes shift in almost unnoticeable increments from Jesus to wealth. I need brothers and sisters in Christ who lovingly but firmly remind me that I am made for better stuff than that. So do you.

Someone said that failure and success are the two greatest impostors. I agree. Most of us think that failure means it's over and success means you have arrived. Nothing could be further from the truth. Even though Nebuchadnezzar failed the test of prosperity initially, that failure became the back door to enduring spiritual prosperity. Each of us can learn through our own failures as well. Who knows what great things God might do through us, once we have learned to pass the test of prosperity?

TIME FOR THOUGHT

1. God interrupts our lives in adversity and in prosperity. Unfortunately we listen more attentively in adversity than in prosperity. Have you ever been tested by prosperity? What happened? _____
_____
_____
_____

DAY TWO: Use the following questions to stimulate your thought.

GROUP LEADER: Discuss these questions in the group after you have read the beginning text aloud together.

2. When things are really going well, it's easy to let things slip. What has a tendency to slip in your life?
   - ❏ Time in the Word
   - ❏ Prayer
   - ❏ Fellowship with other Christians
   - ❏ Worship
   - ❏ Other _____
   _____

3. Have you known anyone who passed the test of prosperity well? Anyone who failed? What did you learn? _____
   _____
   _____
   _____
   _____

4. Read the following verses. What do they tell us about the source of prosperity?
   Ecclesiastes 7:14 _____
   _____
   Psalm 127:1-2 _____
   _____
   Philippians 4:19 _____
   _____
   Deuteronomy 8:10-18 _____
   _____
   Psalm 16:2,5-6,11 _____
   _____
   1 Samuel 2:7 _____
   _____
   Psalm 23:1-2 _____
   _____

5. Read 2 Corinthians 9:6-11. What principles do you find in this passage about prosperity? ___
   _____
   _____

_____
_____
_____
_____

6. In order for us to "take hold of true life" we will have to turn loose of the world. What is it hardest for you to turn loose of? _____
_____
_____
_____
_____
_____

7. Read the following verses and see what you can learn about God's purposes in the gift of prosperity.

DAY FOUR

Ecclesiastes 5:18-19 _____
_____

Proverbs 10:22 _____
_____

1 Timothy 5:8 _____
_____

1 Timothy 5:17-18 _____
_____

1 Corinthians 16:1-2 _____
_____

2 Corinthians 9:12-15 _____
_____

What God's purpose is not:
1 Timothy 6:17-18 _____
_____

James 1:10 _____
_____

Luke 12:15-21 _____
_____

8. Read the following passages and discover what the dangers of prosperity are.

Hosea 13:6 _____

_____

Psalm 49:16-20 _____

_____

Psalm 50:21 _____

_____

Job 12:5; 1 John 3:17 _____

_____

Psalm 16:4; Proverbs 23:4-5 _____

_____

Ecclesiastes 5:10-12 _____

_____

Luke 9:24 _____

_____

9. What steps can you take, beginning now, to pass the test of prosperity? _____

_____

_____

_____

_____

_____

_____

Notes

1. "Tales from the Dark Side of Medicine," *Medical Economics*, November 1998, p. 28-29.
2. The King's malady is not unknown to psychology today. It is a disorder called zoanthropy, in which the victim thinks and behaves like an animal.
3. Stanley W. Angrist, "Selling to the Rich—and to Regular Folk," *The Wall Street Journal,* September 21, 1992; Faith Popcorn, *The Popcorn Report* (New York: Doubleday, 1991), 191.

Session Six

Avoiding
a Wasted Life

King Belshazzar thought he knew the menu for his grand party. He didn't realize that God was serving dessert. As wine brought the temporary illusion of peace, safety, and invincibility to the king and his guests, Cyrus and the Persian army encircled Babylon's impenetrable defenses. Suddenly all grew deathly quiet. Hush settled over the banquet hall as men and women gasped in horror at a supernatural phenomenon before their eyes.

DAY ONE: Read Daniel 5 and pages 67-77.

> Everyone sooner or later sits down to a banquet of consequences.
> —Robert Louis Stevenson

A hand, unconnected to a body, was scratching huge letters into the fresco of Belshazzar's accomplishments on the wall behind the head table. Then, as mysteriously as it came, the hand was gone, leaving only a mysterious message from God and the knocking knees of the king. Courage ran like hot wax from his body, and the powerful king of Babylon collapsed.

When he had recovered sufficiently, the king called in all his advisors. This elite group had failed to connect on two previous occasions under Nebuchadnezzar and were up to the plate for their third swing at deciphering God's message. Now with the very words in front of them, this baffled bunch of baggy-eyed bureaucrats went down swinging—three strikes and they were out. As brilliant as they were, they could not decipher

If any man builds on this foundation using gold, silver, costly stones, wood, hay or straw, his work will be shown for what it is, because the Day will bring it to light. It will be revealed with fire, and the fire will test the quality of each man's work.
—1 Corinthians 3:12-13

67

the message. The privilege of understanding God's mind belongs to those who know Him. Fortunately, there was someone near who knew God well—Daniel.

The queen mother, Nitocris, Nebuchadnezzar's daughter, heard the commotion and came to the king. In so many words, she said, "Pull yourself together and call Daniel. He did it before as chief of your grandfather's advisors, and he can do it again." She should know. She was there. Interestingly, she called Daniel by his Hebrew, not his Babylonian name, which indicates that she knew Daniel personally and probably his God as well.

Though Mothers seem to never give up. There is a time when God says, "Enough." The old hymn reminds us, "Once to every man and nation comes a time when he must choose." That time had come and passed for Belshazzar. He had chosen, all right—chosen judgment, and God's appointed executioner stood outside the city gates. Babylon would fall, however, not because of the enemy without, but the enemy within.

The Enemy Within

After what must have seemed like an eternity, Daniel, the stately octogenarian, marched into the banquet hall, his confidence a stark contrast to the King's cowering. Daniel refused the rewards and rejected the phony words of honor the king offered. Before explaining God's message of judgment, a disgusted Daniel leveled four acerbic charges against King Belshazzar.

(1) The king rejected the truth. After rehearsing Nebuchadnezzar's pilgrimage to faith, Daniel turned to the king and rebuked him. Belshazzar knew the story well and yet had refused to take to heart the solemn warnings God had given. He chose to turn his back on the truth.

But you . . . O Belshazzar, have not humbled yourself, though you knew all this. Instead, you have set yourself up against the Lord of heaven. You had the goblets from his temple brought to you, and you and your nobles, your wives and your concubines drank wine from them. You praised the gods of silver and gold, of bronze, iron, wood and stone, which cannot see or hear or understand. But you did not honor the God who holds in his hand your life and all your ways.
—Daniel 5:22-23

68

(2) The king arrogantly challenged God. Most men are content to just ignore God. Unfortunately, Belshazzar didn't stop there. He defied God to exercise authority over his life when he brought the Temple goblets in, saying in essence, "Stop me if You can." God rarely drops that kind of challenge.

(3) The king worshiped false gods. Given the choice between the one true God and gods who could neither hear nor speak, he chose the latter. Why would someone make that choice? The answer is clear. We don't have to submit to what we create. It serves us.

(4) The king wasted his life. It was incredible to Daniel as he uttered the last charge, "You did not honor the God who holds in his hand your life and all your ways" (v. 23). Belshazzar had wasted his life and missed the purpose of his being. Rather than seeking God's glory, he had lived totally for himself. Now what glory he had would be snuffed out with a swiftness he could not imagine.

Belshazzar is not the only leader who has muscled in on God's glory. Louis XIV had the most magnificent court in Europe. He called himself "Louis the Great." Before he died in 1715, he gave elaborate instructions for the most spectacular funeral ever given a European monarch. A single candle burned on his gold coffin, illuminating the darkness to dramatize his greatness. But as thousands waited in hushed silence, Bishop Massilon approached the coffin, snuffed out the flame, and declared in a voice that echoed through the silent, cavernous cathedral, "Only God is great!"

Silence answered Daniel's charges. He turned and read the four-word inscription:

Mene, Mene, Tekel, Parsin

The message was composed of three Aramaic words: *mene,* meaning to number; *tekel,* to weigh; and *peres,* to divide. Daniel then interpreted:

This is what the words mean:

Mene: God has numbered the days of your reign and brought it to an end.
Tekel: You have been weighed on the scales and found wanting.
Peres: Your kingdom is divided and given to the Medes and Persians.

(Daniel 5:26-28)

We might paraphrase it like this: "Your number is up. You're a moral lightweight—you've squandered your privileges. The party's over."

Literally, it was over. Ironic as it may seem, the last official act of the government of Babylon on October 12, 539 B.C. was to reward the man who proclaimed its demise. There was no repentance, no wailing—just resignation. In a few hours Belshazzar would be dead. Babylon the Great would be assigned its page in history.

The Enemy Without

While the party raged on into the evening, the Persian camp made final preparations for a party of its own for Belshazzar. According to the historian Heroditus, Cyrus, who had already defeated Belshazzar's father, Naboditus, divided his army into three groups. One group gathered at the North, where the Euphrates River entered the city. The second group gathered at the South, where the river exited the city. A third group marched upstream to divert the river into a swamp, making it fordable downstream at the city. The Persian army waded the river and entered Babylon without a fight.

The most powerful empire of the ancient world fell that night without a fight, unable to defend itself against the judgment of God. Not to diminish the Persian force without, Babylon's real enemy was within. Unlike his grandfather, Belshazzar proved irresponsible with God's rev-

A man who remains stiff-necked after many rebukes will suddenly be destroyed—without remedy.
—Proverbs 29:1

elation, wasted his life, and suffered the irreversible consequences. The same can happen to any person, profession, or culture that turns away from the truth.

When I read this chapter, I can't help but wonder how close we are to God's judgment. At some point we may go too far, setting in motion events as impossible to change as delaying the sunset on that fateful day twenty-five-hundred years ago in Babylon.

> A good many people fret themselves over the rather improbable speculation that the earth may be blown asunder by nuclear weapons. The grimmer and more immediate prospect is that men and women may be reduced to a sub-human state through limitless indulgence in their own vices—with ruinous consequences to society.
> —Russell Kirk

Is the Sun Setting on Hippocratic Medicine?

Ominous shadows are falling across our great land, and many social critics are predicting a new "dark age" as western civilization falters under the attack of a new breed of barbarian. The Goths and Vandals of our present age are not the crazed, drunken invaders from without, but polished, persuasive, pleasant men and women from within who have rejected the truth. Scandal follows our leaders like a bad dream. Everywhere men and women trade convictions for cash, sacrifice integrity on the altar of success, and allow greed to eclipse character.

> Then they will know that I am the LORD, when I have made the land a desolate waste because of all the detestable things they have done.
> —Ezekiel 33:29

I would like to say that this darkness has not affected medicine, but unfortunately, medical science has been at the forefront of some of America's knottiest debates—and politicians follow where medicine leads.

The value of human life, the foundation of Hippocratic medicine, has been eroded. Three days into his new administration, Bill Clinton took pen in hand and issued four executive orders lifting a degree of restraint in our growing disregard for life:

1. The ban on using "fetal tissue" for medical research was lifted.
2. The ban on abortion counseling in federally funded clinics was rescinded.
3. The importation process of the controversial abortion-inducing drug, RU 486, was begun.
4. Funding for abortions in military hospitals overseas was provided.

Our culture is facing a threat of colossal proportion that could mean the end of medicine as we know it. It is not solely the dangers of managed care, genetic engineering, or euthanasia. It's the character of the men and women unbridled by truth.

The spiritual disease that plagued ancient Babylon is roaring unchecked through medicine. For over two thousand years, medical concepts of right and wrong rested firmly on the teaching of Hippocrates and Judeo-Christian tradition. In the vacuum left by the banishment of spiritual truth, a new, selfish individualism has taken the seat of ascendancy. Holding to biblical ideas of right and wrong today, however, will get you scorned, laughed at, pitied, and sometimes attacked.

> We have reached a point in history when the unchecked pursuit of truth, without regard to its social consequences, will bring to a swift end the pursuit of truth . . . by wiping out the very civilization that has favored it. That would indeed be the judgment of God.
>
> —Lewis Mumford

Make no mistake, we are in a battle for the heart and soul of medicine. The fact is that no group or person who rejects God and His Word will escape His judgment. If we continue to walk in the darkness and presume on God's patience, we should expect God's judgment. Perhaps managed care and the multiplication of malpractice suits have been wake-up calls.

Don't misunderstand me. I don't believe the cause is lost. Listen to Dr. David Stevens, executive director of the Christian Medical and Dental Society:

> The gulf between what medicine is and what we should be is alarming. If we as doctors continue to focus on pleasing ourselves, someone will steal our profession and our freedom; and we'll have no one to blame but ourselves. But I'm hopeful that God is at work changing the face of healthcare by changing the hearts of doctors—one life at a time. The demise of medicine is inevitable only if doctors refuse to let God change them from the inside out.

How to Avoid a Wasted Life

Like it or not, God holds each of us responsible for all we do. Paul said, "Do not be deceived: God cannot be mocked. A man reaps what he sows" (Galatians 6:7). Notice that this warning is given to individuals, not societies, though it is certainly applicable to the latter. If we are able to turn back the barbarians, it will be because men and women like you walk into the light, one person at a time. And because you do so not with bullhorns and slogans, but with a personal righteousness that others cannot deny.

> Responsibility is the high price of self-ownership.
> —Eli J. Schleifer

Otherwise, we will fare no better than Belshazzar. We will waste life, pursuing personal peace and prosperity at the expense of God's glory. How can we avoid that kind of waste?

Listen carefully to God. Never before in the history of the world has the Word of God been so freely accessible to God's people. With this abundant privilege comes a tremendous responsibility—the responsibility of listening carefully and obeying.

When I read about Daniel and Belshazzar in Daniel 5, I think of the contrast in Psalm 1.

> Blessed is the man who does not walk
>   in the counsel of the wicked
> or stand in the way of sinners
>   or sit in the seat of scoffers
> But his delight is in the law of the LORD,
>   and on his law he meditates day and night.
> He is like a tree planted by streams of water,
>   which yields its fruit in season
> and whose leaf does not wither.
>   Whatever he does prospers.
> Not so the wicked!
>   They are like chaff
>   that the wind blows away.
>   (Psalm 1:1-4)

What is God trying to say to you and me? Are we listening? Every one of us needs the constant communication that God makes available to us through His Word. As Psalm 1 says, we need to meditate on God's Word—read it, then think about its meaning and application to every part of our lives. The images and messages that constantly bombard us need evaluation. When the message of our culture and the Word of God call us in differ-

---

It is time to start reclaiming the most powerful weapon we have against the darkness. A weapon that seems to have suffered as we have picketed and politicked as though revival comes through governmental power. This weapon is the weapon of individual proclamation of light. . . . It is ignited not through public policy statements but rather in and through individual lives that are nonnegotiably committed to thinking and living from a biblical point of view.

—Joe Stowell
The Dawn's Early Light

ent directions, we must choose. We can't ride the fence or incise our lives into spiritual and secular, pretending to obey God at home and at church, while living by another set of rules in our work.

What I do with God's Word determines whether I become a lightweight like Belshazzar—easily toppled by the winds of change and adversity—or a strong, stable individual like Daniel—firmly planted in the truth.

Don't move the goal line. Imagine a football game where the goal line was constantly moving. You would have eleven frustrated defensive players not knowing what they were defending and eleven offensive players not knowing where they had to go to succeed. A sport like that would lose popularity fast, but in the realm of medical ethics that is exactly what is going on. Every time we turn around, we have a new criterion of what's acceptable and what's not.

Once considered a horror by almost every American, abortion has been embraced as the most convenient way to deal with unwanted pregnancies. Lack of respect for life at its beginning has led in due course to questions about the value of life at its end. Now a growing number of doctors embrace physician-assisted suicide and euthanasia, anathema to the Hippocratic tradition, as treatment options. Genetic engineering that would have made Hitler's doctors salivate is becoming available faster than we can consider its consequences. Our new favorite criterion for decision making is asking only, "Is it possible,

> No, the crisis that threatens us, the force that could topple our monuments and destroy our very foundation, is within ourselves. The crisis is in the character of our culture, where the values that restrain inner vices and develop inner virtues are eroding. Unprincipled men and women, disdainful of their moral heritage and skeptical of Truth itself, are destroying our civilization by weakening the very pillars upon which it rests.
>
> —Chuck Colson
> *Against the Night*

and will it make life easier and more convenient?"

Live in humility. Giving God the place in our lives that He actually occupies in the universe is the first order of business for all of God's creatures. That He has given us a choice is at once a great mystery and precisely why we can have a person-to-person relationship with Him. As a person, I can choose to live life on my own or under His lordship.

The wonderful thing about submitting ourselves to Christ is that not only do we avoid God's judgment, but we experience all of His richness in the abundant life of Jesus.

Never give up. Our job, of course, is not to change medicine, but to be faithful to God, to pray for our communities (Jeremiah 29:11-12), to graciously confront sin when necessary, and to call men and women to repentance (Daniel 4:27). If Daniel's life reminds us of anything, it is that even the godliest of lives cannot guarantee the salvation of a culture from judgment. But good men and women can make a difference for good, and individual lives can be changed. We never know, however, when a sovereign God might pick us up and use us as He did Daniel. Therefore, we need to be ready.

Oswald Chambers challenges us to view God's power as a river. He reminds us that there are times, because of some obstacle, we can't see that we are any use at all. In times like these, when we seem to lack influence, we need to keep our focus on the Source of life, not the obstacle. Chambers says, "The obstacle is a matter of in-

> I have come that they may have life, and have it to the full.
> —John 10:10

The cost of nondiscipleship is incredibly high: "Abiding peace, a life penetrated throughout by love, faith that sees everything in the light of God's overriding governance for good, hopefulness that stands firm in the most discouraging of circumstances, power to do what is right and withstand the forces of evil. In short, it costs exactly that abundance of life Jesus said he came to bring."
—Dallas Willard
The Spirit of the Disciplines

---

difference to the river which will flow steadily through you if you remember to keep right at the Source."[1]

During the times we wonder what God is doing, we need to bear down on our relationship with Jesus, not the removal of the obstacle. We can allow nothing to come between Christ and us. If we keep our channel to the Source open and unconstricted, we can be sure rivers of living water will flow into us and then spring up, changing others.

> Our goal is to be faithful to the holy God who calls us to be the church, whether we actually make a difference in our world or whether it falls to pieces around us and dissolves into a stew of secularism.
>
> —Chuck Colson

TIME FOR THOUGHT

1. How was Belshazzar similar to Nebuchadnezzar? _____
   _____
   _____
   _____

   How was he different? _____
   _____
   _____
   _____
   _____
   _____
   _____

2. In your opinion, is the medical establishment more like Nebuchadnezzar, Belshazzar, or Daniel? Why do you think this? _____
   _____
   _____
   _____
   _____

DAY TWO: Use the following questions to stimulate your thought.

GROUP LEADER: Discuss these questions in the group after you have read the beginning text aloud together.

3. Look back at Daniel's attitude toward Belshazzar. Contrast his attitude toward Nebuchadnezzar. How is it different? _____

_____

_____

_____

What reason can you give? _____

_____

_____

_____

4. How should you respond to a person like Belshazzar today? Why? Under what circumstances would your answer change?
   ❑ Avoid him and let him go to hell. _____

   _____

   ❑ Confront him and try to change him. _____

   _____

   ❑ Rebuke him as Daniel did. _____

   _____

   ❑ Other _____

   _____

5. Read Proverbs 21:11. What can we learn from others' mistakes? _____

_____

_____

What if we don't? _____

_____

_____

6. The Bible is clear about our responsibility to respond to what we know—revelation brings responsibility. Why is this important? _____

_____

_____

_____

Read John 3:10-12. What principle does Jesus teach Nicodemus? _____

_____

_____

_____

7. One of Belshazzar's problems was that he chose to worship other gods when he knew better. What do you think motivates men and women to worship gods of their own making?
   ☐ Ignorance
   ☐ Tradition
   ☐ Convenience
   ☐ Manipulation
   ☐ Other _____

   Why is it so dangerous? _____

   _____

   _____

   _____

8. Read Psalm 1 again. Think about it for a minute: from whom or what have you taken advice lately?
   ☐ A skeptic   ☐ A wise person
   ☐ A scoffer   ☐ A fool
   ☐ A sinner   ☐ A good book
   ☐ A godly person   ☐ The Bible
   ☐ Other _____

   _____

   According to Psalm 1, what are the benefits of rooting yourself deep in God's Word? _____

   _____

   _____

   _____

   _____

   _____

   _____

9. How real is God's Word to you?
   - ❑ Very real
   - ❑ Sometimes meaningful
   - ❑ Mostly irrelevant
   - ❑ Other _____

   Is there a verse you can share with others in the group that is especially meaningful to you?

   _____
   _____

10. How have you used God's Word practically since you've been in medical school? _____

    _____
    _____

    Is there a method or way you study or read the Bible that is especially helpful to you that you can share? _____

    _____
    _____

Notes

1. Oswald Chambers, *My Utmost for His Highest* (New York: Dodd, Mead & Co., 1935), 250.

How to Sleep with Lions without Being Eaten

The threat of a malpractice suit is a reality for every practicing doctor. Though only one out of ten cases filed goes to court, even the thought of being sued has a chilling affect on most physicians. A sense of fear, betrayal, loss of confidence, anger, withdrawal, and family conflict can all result from a call from an attorney. Perhaps worst of all, you can begin to view your patients as potential adversaries rather than as the men and women God sent you to serve.

DAY ONE: Read Daniel 5:31-6:28 and pages 81-89.

> When I was named as a codefendant in a lawsuit some time ago, I was devastated. The patient-plaintiff was one for whom I had been consulted. I had given her scrupulous care. Her family and I were on the best of terms. Her granddaughter was even my office nurse!
>
> Over time, I became less accessible to those around me. I began to look at my patients as potential litigants. My wife and children suffered as my "fuse" shortened and my temperament hardened.
>
> —Dr. Curtis E. Harris
> *Today's Christian Doctor*

Whether an attack is professional or personal, such encounters tend to make a person wonder whether the monks didn't have a pretty good idea—find a remote cave and shut yourself off where no one can hurt you. There are two problems with the isolation approach. First, God has called us to fully engage the world, not retreat from it. Second, as long as we are on this earth, we can count on Satan to stir up strife. Any cave we choose is just as likely to be a lions' den as

For more information about CMDA's Medical Malpractice Ministry, please call 888-230-2637.

the hospital. We will never reach a point in life—spiritually, vocationally, or socially—where we can expect smooth sailing. As long as we walk this planet, the potential of an attack is always present. This is especially true if we attempt to live for Christ.

When Life Bites

At eighty-plus, Daniel had no notion of taking the easy road around potential lions. As Israel's seventy-year captivity came to a close, Daniel knew this was no time to shrink from his responsibility to serve God and his fellow man. Even though it would have been easy for him to play it safe, Daniel again accepted a prominent place in public service when the new Persian government took over.

Verse 31 of Daniel 5 marks an historic transition. On October 12, 539 B.C., Belshazzar reigned as King of Babylon. On October 13, "Darius the Mede" took over the kingdom at the age of sixty-two. In this capacity under Cyrus, King of Persia, Darius immediately began to reorganize the government of Babylon. He appointed 120 satraps to rule over various parts of the kingdom. Over these individuals, Darius appointed three administrators, including Daniel, to protect the King's interests.

		Commissioner 1 →	40 Satraps
Cyrus →	Darius →	Commissioner 2 →	40 Satraps
		Daniel →	40 Satraps

Think about it a moment: new boss, new staff, new responsibilities, new procedures, new culture. Add an eighty-plus-year-old-government official brought out of retirement. Would you really expect to read of Daniel's outstanding performance? Note the three things we learn about Daniel.

First, he was *competent*. The words "distinguished himself" translated literally from the Ara-

Now Daniel so distinguished himself among the administrators and satraps by his exceptional qualities that the king planned to set him over the whole kingdom.

—Daniel 6:3

maic mean "to show one's self prominent." Daniel did excellent work. In fact, he did it decidedly better than anyone else. Over the years God had moved him into a position that fully utilized his God-given core competencies. Rather than drain him, Daniel's work enthused and invigorated him because he was able to do what God had created him to do. As a result of this, no one could keep up with Daniel even in his eighties.

Second, Daniel was a man of *character*. "Exceptional qualities" characterized Daniel. Unfortunately, many individuals fear that godly character makes them very vulnerable in the dog-eat-dog environment of the workplace. This would be true if Jesus Christ was not present as the Lord of the workplace. Daniel faced every bit as hostile an environment as any of us faces today, and he found God faithful to protect him.

Third, Daniel had an incredible *capacity*. Not only was he able to handle one-third of the entire province of Babylon, Daniel was about to be awarded authority over the entire kingdom. This was no small assignment—Babylon covered a land mass roughly half the size of the United States.

Daniel's competence, character, and capacity for work opened doors to greater opportunities for influence, but they did not deliver him from attack. Unfortunately, not everyone wants to celebrate our successes.

The Conspiracy

As soon as Daniel's peers heard of the King's plan to promote him, they determined to sabotage his success. With probability on their side, they reasoned that any government official who had been around as long as Daniel must have a few skeletons in the closet somewhere. The Bible tells us what they found—nothing! They monitored his bank accounts, audited his books, checked

> Therefore, I urge you, brothers, in view of God's mercy, to offer your bodies as living sacrifices, holy and pleasing to God—this is your spiritual act of worship. Do not conform any longer to the pattern of this world, but be transformed by the renewing of your mind. Then you will be able to test and approve what God's will is—his good, pleasing and perfect will.
> —Romans 12:1-2

the document shredder (or cuneiform crusher, as it would have been). He was not misusing the palace post office, writing hot checks, or sexually harassing his office staff. There were no bribes, no cover-ups, no scandals. The only evidence they found confirmed the wisdom of Darius's decision to promote Daniel.

If Nebuchadnezzar and Belshazzar failed the test of prosperity, Daniel passed with flying colors. At the pinnacle of his career, publicly and privately, he was the same man—a man of impeccable integrity. Drawing a double blank in Daniel's public and private affairs, his enemies knew they would have to somehow trump him regarding his faith.

Appealing to Darius's pride, the administrators and satraps tricked him into creating a law they knew Daniel would violate because of his commitment to God. In a show of solidarity, the conspirators sought an audience with the new king and presented their request.

With the transition to the Persian government, the proposed law seemed to be a good idea—a sort of pledge of allegiance to their new country. Obviously, it was also an ego trip for Darius. Taking the bait, he signed the order, making it irrevocable law, before he thought things through.

Daniel's Consistency
What happened next shouldn't surprise me, but it does. Daniel's raw integrity seems almost outrageous in our culture, one that smirks at honor and is so used to hypocrisy and scandal in high places that no one seems to care.

As I see it, Daniel had three choices: cease to pray; close the window and pray in secret; pray

At this, the administrators and satraps tried to find grounds for charges against Daniel in his conduct of government affairs, but they were unable to do so. They could find no corruption in him, because he was trustworthy and neither corrupt nor negligent. Finally these men said, "We will never find any basis for charges against this man Daniel unless it has something to do with the law of his God."
—Daniel 6:4-5

We make men without chests and expect of them virtue and enterprise. We laugh at honour and are shocked to find traitors in our midst.
—C. S. Lewis

as usual. Each choice had a tremendous price tag. Weighing the costs, Daniel put his life on the line rather than sacrifice either God's glory or God's fellowship on the altar of security. He prayed "just as he had done before."

Darius's response—"great distress"— is surprising in the context of the angry, arrogant kings we have encountered previously. But in the short time they had worked together, Darius had developed a deep respect and love for this eighty-year-old exile.

Love demanded forgiveness. Justice demanded retribution. There was no way of escape for Darius. Recognizing that he was powerless, Darius did the only thing left. He hoped against all his sixty-two years of pagan experience that the God in whom Daniel had absolute confidence could deliver him.

Sleepless in Babylon

As the huge stone was rolled into position covering the mouth of the den, the conspirators went home to celebrate and Darius went to his palace to mourn.

Since the Bible follows Darius rather than Daniel, we know what happened in the palace, but we are left to our imagination as to Daniel's night. Doubt brought disquiet and anxiety to the palace, but faith brought rest to the lions' den. The first light of day found Darius at the back at the door of Daniel's prison. Overjoyed at his friend's survival, Darius ordered Daniel lifted out of the den. He didn't have a scratch on him because as the Bible adds, "he had trusted in his God" (6:23).

Daniel 6 is the last historical chapter of the book and includes an amazing tribute to this man of faith. It is not a commendation of Daniel that outlined his feats of faith and service to the king. Instead we find a royal decree from a man whom

Now when Daniel learned that the decree had been published, he went home to his upstairs room where the windows opened toward Jerusalem. Three times a day he got down on his knees and prayed, giving thanks to his God, just as he had done before.
—Daniel 6:10

Daniel influenced greatly, praising the character and wonders of Daniel's God, and calling on all men to do the same.

Surviving the Lions

Daniel provides an excellent paradigm for not only facing but also surviving an attack, whether it is a frivolous malpractice suit or an attack of jealous peers.

Lessons from the Den

Do quality work. Both our ability to positively impact others and our ability to survive attack depends on our competence. A great deal of confusion exists among Christians about the place of our everyday work in God's plan. As far as God is concerned, our most basic responsibility in serving Him is doing our work with excellence. Whether our work finds us in a hospital or a government office, as in the case of Daniel, God wants us to pursue excellence.

Everyone makes mistakes, and every doctor provides substandard care at some point. We're all human. But nothing is more discrediting to your Christian witness and mine than consistent mediocrity in our work. The first thing the men and women around us will notice is the quality of our labor. Follow Daniel's example—don't give them anything to criticize.

Make faithfulness your highest priority. No other goal is lofty or compelling enough to energize you to keep going when you are facing the lions. Notice that Daniel didn't go on the attack himself—and I'm sure he could have. Getting even is a sidetrack unworthy of a Christian.

Be self-controlled and alert. Your enemy the devil prowls around like a roaring lion looking for someone to devour. Resist him, standing firm in the faith, because you know your brothers throughout the world are undergoing the same sufferings.
—1 Peter 5:8-9

Nothing is more dangerous to the faith of youth than for them to make the disconcerting discovery that the men who have advocated their faith are men of mediocre ability.
—Frank Gabelein

Daniel didn't even try to defend himself. He let his reputation speak for itself and he kept at his job as a faithful administrator and disciple.

Don't be surprised when attacked. Lions don't live just in dens. They work in offices and live in neighborhoods and even go to churches just like yours. Peter warns us, "Do not be surprised at the painful trial you are suffering, as though something strange were happening to you" (1 Peter 4:12). Even Christ warned us to expect attack.

> The greatest evil is not done in those sordid "dens of crime" that Dickens loved to paint. . . . It is conceived and . . . moved, seconded, carried, and minuted . . . in clean, carpeted, warmed, and well-lighted offices, by quiet men with white collars and cut fingernails and smooth-shaven cheeks who do not need to raise their voices.
>
> —C. S. Lewis
> *The Screwtape Letters*

Maintain an attitude of thanksgiving. One of the items so easily missed in this dramatic story is found in Daniel 6:10: Daniel continued giving thanks to his God. What would you have done? Knowing the plot was hatched, knowing enemies were watching, knowing there was no way anyone could save you, would you be occupied with the goodness of God?

Thanksgiving is not only an act of gratitude, it is an expression of faith. Because I know God has given His peace and protection even though I may not feel or see them at the moment, I can thank the Lord for these things. This is not pretending, but acknowledging spiritual reality. Because He can do "exceeding abundantly beyond what I ask or think," I can thank the Lord for strength and endurance when I feel like I can't go on. Because I know His love is ready to flow through me at that very moment, and He's the one who said, "Father, forgive them, for they do not know what they are doing," I can thank the Lord for the ability to love when I am being attacked and want to attack in return.

> Let the peace of Christ rule in your hearts, since as members of one body you were called to peace. And be thankful.
> —Colossians 3:15

Thanksgiving turns my attention to the Source of my life and reminds me of the abundance I have in Christ. It frees my mind and emotions from the resources of this world that someone may be trying to take away and lifts me into the abundant storehouse of God.

Never let the enemy set the agenda. Don't play by their rules—play by God's rules. I am convinced that Daniel could have eaten his opponents alive, but he refused to live by their rules, where anything goes and the ends justify the means. Peter reminds us of the Christian's rules when he writes, "Do not repay evil for evil or insult with insult, but with blessing."

Put your reputation in God's hands. Margaret Thatcher, former prime minister of Great Britain, had wise words when she said, "Being powerful is like being a lady. If you have to tell people you are, you aren't." That's true of anyone's reputation. If you are innocent, you don't need to broadcast it. The more you protest, the worse you look. As Shakespeare said, "Me thinks the lady doth protest too much." When Daniel came under attack, he kept quiet—and kept at his routine.

Maintain consistency. Changing your routine makes you look guilty whether you are or not. Under pressure, I've found that it's easy to trim back a little on integrity. Faced with criticism, it's natural to conform.

Don't resist alone. Even here where it ap-

> Do not repay evil for evil or insult with insult, but with blessing, because to this you were called so that you may inherit a blessing. For,
> "Whoever would love life
>   and see good days
> must keep his tongue from evil
>   and his lips from evil speech.
> He must turn from evil and do good;
>   he must seek peace and pursue it.
> For the eyes of the Lord are on the
>   righteous and his ears are attentive
>   to their prayer,
> but the face of the Lord is against
>   those who do evil."
> —1 Peter 3:9-12

pears Daniel must stand alone, a second look will reveal a compatriot—King Darius. Very likely Daniel had outlived Shadrach, Meshach, Abednego, and most of the other men of faith who had come from Judah seventy years before. But as we see in this chapter, Daniel was consistently making new acquaintances and expanding his friendships. Unlike many older individuals whose circle of friends and supporters shrinks, Daniel's was growing. Not only did these people need Daniel, but Daniel needed them. We lean on each other, carry each other, and even stand on each other's shoulders, together becoming what God wants us to be and bringing glory to His name.

TIME FOR THOUGHT

1. Do you know anyone who has experienced a malpractice suit? What was the outcome? How did it impact the doctor? _____
_____
_____
_____

DAY TWO: Use the following questions to stimulate your thought.

GROUP LEADER: Discuss these questions in the group after you have read the beginning text aloud together.

2. How do most people respond when attacked? Why do you think this is true? _____
_____
_____
_____

3. According to the experts, there are things a doctor can do to avoid malpractice suits. Read 1 Corinthians 4:12-13. What kind of advice might Paul give a doctor today? _____
_____
_____
_____

4. Has anyone ever been jealous of your work or an honor you've received? What happened?

_____

_____

_____

_____

_____

_____

5. Read the following verses. What strategies do they suggest for responding to attacks?

Romans 12:18-21 _____

_____

_____

1 Peter 2:15-16 _____

_____

_____

1 Peter 2:20-22 _____

_____

_____

1 Peter 3:9-12 _____

_____

_____

Why is it best to keep quiet when someone attacks you? _____

_____

_____

_____

6. Have you ever seen a non-Christian defend a Christian? What can you learn from Daniel and Darius's relationship that would explain why that might happen? _____

_____

_____

_____

_____

7. Read 1 Peter 4:12-14. Why do attacks surprise us? _____
_____
_____

What good can come out of hard times? _____
_____
_____

8. Why is thanksgiving so important for men and women who want to follow Christ? _____
_____
_____
_____
_____

Have you ever been able to give thanks in a time of difficulty? When? _____
_____
_____
_____

DAY FIVE

9. In the midst of a difficult time, have you ever had someone support you and remind you of the spiritual reality you can be thankful for? What happened? _____
_____
_____
_____
_____

How important is it to have someone like that in medical school? _____
_____
_____

When you enter practice? _____
_____
_____

10. Dr. Curt Harris suggests several ways to help a colleague who has been attacked by the malpractice lion. See if these don't make sense to you, as you look to the future:

❑ Call your colleague as soon as you learn about the case. Physicians generally isolate themselves when stressed.

❑ Listen to his or her feelings. You do not need to have a wise answer. Simply listening is enough.

❑ Ask him how the case is going—in private.

❑ Remember that he or she likely will suffer from feelings of inadequacy.

❑ Offer your prayer support and then do pray.

❑ Avoid chattering about malpractice lawyers.

❑ Refrain from encouraging a countersuit.

Becoming a Person of Influence

No one even remotely in touch with current events could have missed the news coverage of "Magic" Johnson's announcement that he was HIV positive. It was a media circus. The morning of November 9, 1991, CNN coverage aired successive clips of Johnson's press conference, Pat Riley praying for Johnson with the Lakers, President Bush's public statement of personal concern, and a report that the CDC in Atlanta had been deluged with ten thousand calls an hour about AIDS since the Thursday announcement.

DAY ONE: Reread Daniel 1 and 6 and pages 93-106.

Why does one person's tragedy affect so many people? Certainly AIDS is no backwater issue. It seems almost every Hollywood star is an AIDS spokesperson or fund-raiser. But everyone from Health Department officials to those lobbying for AIDS research funding predicted a massive increase in awareness because of the plight of this one person. The reason is that Earvin Johnson is a person of influence. And whether we like it or not, Johnson was influenc-

> It's easier to make a fortune than to make a difference.

ing the moral values of our nation in the early nineties—perhaps even more than the church.

The withdrawal of the church from significant interaction with our culture during the larger part of this century has left a vacuum of influence in our culture that secular people have only been too glad to fill. As we consider how to regain lost influence, particularly in medicine, the Book of Daniel has given us some clear insights. In his seventy-plus years of service, Daniel exerted a consistent influence in the Babylonian and Persian governments that not only changed the lives of individuals but the course of history as well. It was under his watch that the first exiles returned to Israel.

We often think of influential individuals like Daniel as people of destiny. They seem to appear almost magically in history at precisely the right time. In recent history, figures such as George Washington, Abraham Lincoln, William Wilberforce, and Winston Churchill come to mind. In our own day, John Kennedy, Billy Graham, Martin Luther King Jr., and Mother Teresa all seem to be individuals of destiny. A close examination of their lives, however, reveals that they were all just ordinary people who were exercising the disciplines of influence on a micro level. They had a destiny for influence before God dropped them in a bigger pond for macro impact. Very likely, if we had approached them during their early lives and suggested that they would become enormously influential, they probably would have laughed and said, "But I'm just doing my job!"

In God's plan, each of us has a destiny. Though the world may never know your name or mine, we have a calling to influence our generation and our profession for Christ. The individuals

George Gallup quantified the loss of influence in his research. He found those believing "religion" is losing influence in America has grown from 14 percent to 49 percent in the last thirty years. Although Gallup found that the U.S. is still a religious country, the sincerity of faith evidenced in his research does not impress him. He wrote, "While religion is highly popular in our country, survey evidence suggests that it is only superficial—it does not change people's lives to the degree one would expect from the level of professed faith."[1]

in the early church understood this well. By the end of the first century the followers of Christ had grown from a few hundred to an estimated five hundred thousand. Thousands of men and women took the gospel with them wherever they went. From this group, God elevated a few we can call by name: Peter, Paul, Barnabus, and John. But even these were ordinary men who took the will of God seriously, no matter how big a pond their rippling influence disturbed.

What Is Influence?

Influence is the power or capacity to produce a desired result, to impact or to cause some change to take place. Rather than focusing on laws, influence focuses on hearts. Although both

> The most important single influence in the life of a person is another person . . . who is worthy of emulation.
> —Paul D. Shafer

involve power, the power of influence is granted rather than imposed. The power of influence given to Magic Johnson, for instance, was conferred by willing people from their hearts. Because of this, influence changes people from the inside out. It sways their thoughts, their perceptions, and their values. As a result, influence also has the power to change behavior.

Recognizing this, Madison Avenue has paid Johnson millions of dollars to influence the public's behavior—to buy certain products. Interestingly, stock shares of Carter-Wallace, maker of Trojan condoms, went up three dollars at the news that Johnson would become a spokesman for safe sex.[2]

Where does this kind of power come from? What is the source of influence? Why does Magic Johnson hold the power to sway our thinking and behavior? We might be tempted to assume that the influence is in the profession itself. It's true that today in America some careers, including professional sports as well as medicine, do provide more of an opportunity for influence than, say, plumbing. But there is more to being influential than your choosing to be a doctor.

The Source of Influence

Throughout the Book of Daniel, God's formula for influence unfolds. Far from resting on one factor, several elements emerge that must come together.

Influence Requires Competence

The foundational first requirement for influence is brut competence—the pursuit of excellence in one's daily work. Scripture lends credence to this idea. Proverbs 22:29 states, "Do you see a man skilled in his work? He will serve before kings; he will not serve before obscure men." Paul commanded us, "Whatever you do, work at it with all your heart" (Colossians 3:23).

> If a man is called to be a street sweeper, he should sweep streets even as Michelangelo painted, or Beethoven composed music, or Shakespeare wrote poetry. He should sweep streets so well that all the hosts of heaven and earth will pause to say, here lived a great street sweeper who did his job well.
> —Martin Luther King Jr.

Influence involves more than choosing a strategic career. The career may provide the opportunity, but influence in that career requires that we do the job well. The public does not give the power of influence for instance to everyone who plays professional sports. The factor that confers the power of influence is excellence. Even among the talented ranks of the NBA, benchwarmers do not interest Madison Avenue—it's the standouts. It's the prodigious ability to turn in an outstanding performance that makes them influential. And it's their excellent performance in an influential career that makes them extremely valuable to those who want to influence behavior, namely the buying habits of the American public.

Consider the lack of impact Daniel would have had on Nebuchadnezzar or Darius had he been mediocre at what he did. Neither of these men would have been inclined to listen to Daniel had he not been a superb administrator. Nebuchadnezzar found no servants equal to Daniel and his friends. Seventy years later, Darius confronted the same competence. What's true in athletics and politics is certainly true in medicine.

Competence requires natural gifts. Hard work doesn't produce competence in a vacuum. It's the disciplined exercise of God-given talent that produces excellence. Not just anyone who works hard can make the NBA. It takes a gift. What is obvious in the realm of professional sports is also true in medicine.

When individuals operate in the realm of their core competencies, they excel, because they are energized and receive a great deal of satisfaction from what they do. But when they ignore their design, there is a predictable scenario of mediocrity and burnout. If the impact were merely personal, it would be bad enough. But it is not. Mediocrity drastically affects our impact on others. To put it bluntly, people don't care if you are a good person until they know you are a good doctor.

> Whatever your hand finds to do, do it with all your might.
> —Ecclesiastes 9:10

GIFT + DISCIPLINE = COMPETENCE

Competence requires discipline. Another factor crucial to the paradigm of influence is responsible action. God may give the gifts, but we must still choose to discover, develop, and employ those gifts. Culture may provide the opportunities for us to touch vast numbers of people, but we must still choose to endure the discipline of craftsmanship to seize the opportunity. That's exactly what you are doing right now in your medical training. It's essential that you work hard to develop the God-given abilities you have to be a good doctor.

We came face-to-face with this necessity in our initial introduction to Daniel. He and his friends were gifted—intellectually superior. But that was not enough. Their gifts had to be developed, and they humbly endured three grueling years of disciplined study. Daniel was faithful to develop what God had given him. No wonder we read at the end of Daniel 1, "And Daniel remained there [in the King's court] until the first year of King Cyrus" (Daniel 1:21).

Influence Requires Character

Competence is only half of the influence equation. Another equally important factor of influence is character. Great character must govern great gift if we want to maintain influence gained by competent work. Lack of integrity has aborted the influence of many a leader. Notable modern examples include Richard Nixon and Bill Clinton, both brilliant, competent men with flawed character.

> COMPETENCE + CHARACTER = AUTHORITY

On the other side are figures of virtue like Billy Graham and Dr. C. Everett Koop. Their integrity over the years has made even their toughest critics respect and admire them. Authentic Christ-likeness consistently impresses people.

Competence and character, when combined, produce an authority that no one can take away. The excellent doctor who is growing in Christ is without a doubt one of the most potent influences for the kingdom of God in our culture.

Influence Requires Courage

As a person accepts the discipline of development and craftsmanship, God may incrementally open greater opportunities of influence. In some instances, God may catapult men and women to totally new levels of influence they never dreamed of. Take Joseph, for example—a young man who graduated from the school of incarceration to become prime minister of Egypt. Esther was a nice Jewish girl whom God had gifted with an abundance of grace and beauty. Suddenly she found herself Queen of Persia and had the opportunity to intervene in her people's annihilation. Daniel was a faithful young man abruptly yanked from his home to eventually become the most enduring political influence in the ancient Near East. In each case, these individuals were devoted to the Lord on a micro level. But moving to macro influence requires courage.

> Soaring never just happens. It is the result of a strong mental effort—thinking clearly, courageously, confidently. No one ever oozed his way out of mediocrity like a slug.
> —Chuck Swindoll

Each of these "promotions" required a large measure of courage to respond to the opportunity. I shudder to think what would have happened to the nation of Israel if men and women like these had followed the modern trend toward a "privatized faith"—personally engaging, but culturally irrelevant. We must reengage the culture on its turf, master its wisdom, face its challenges, and better it. As it did for Daniel, Esther, Joseph, and anyone who has been in a similar situation, this will take a major dose of courage. It takes courage because when we enter the big time, Satan will

> COMPETENCE + CHARACTER + COURAGE = INFLUENCE

not sit by and offer merely token resistance. We can expect opposition such as we have never experienced before. Only one thing stands at that point between us and our destiny—fear.

Discovering Your Destiny

If you want to fulfill your destiny and become a person of influence, it is apparent that you must follow hard after three things.

1. Discover your core competencies and strive for excellence.

Interestingly, when we think of men and women doing God's work today, we think of spiritual activities such as prayer, Bible study, and evangelism as capturing God's interest and pleasure. To be a real spiritual influence, we assume, one has to choose vocational ministry. But how many people see their daily work as something valuable to God, the place of greatest spiritual influence for His kingdom?

More often than not, we find men and women laboring under the assumption that their daily work means very little to God. One physician told me he grew up in a church that had a clear ranking system that looked like this:

    ★★★★   Missionaries
      ★★★   Pastors
        ★★   Bible college attendees

If you were working in a "secular" job and had not been to Bible college, you were doomed to be a lowly "one-star Christian."

If Christ is calling me to make an impact on my world, where is He leading? If the above value system is valid, then choosing a career in medicine, or any other career outside vocational ministry, is a colossal waste of time. I'm glad Daniel and millions of others down through history have resisted this tripe. When William Wilberforce made a serious commitment to Christ, he went to John Newton to discuss whether he should leave Parliament and go to seminary. Newton wisely reminded him, "Maybe God has you there for a purpose." Indeed He did. Wilberforce not only became one of the strongest forces for Christ in his generation, but millions live as free men and women today because of his personal crusade to end slavery in the British empire.

God's will—the place of my greatest fulfillment and joy, greatest competence, and greatest influence—is essentially and fundamentally being what He made me to be. If we think that the only way we can follow God fully is by going into vocational ministry, most of us will miss our destiny as the young man or woman who becomes a doctor. We please God primarily by being what He designed us to be, using the unique set of God-given abilities He put in each of us.

What everyone needs to ask is not "What do I want to do, and what do I have to do to get it?" but "What am I designed to be, and how do I develop what God has already put in me?" If our lives have meaning and purpose, it is reasonable to assume that God shaped our being to accommodate His purpose for our lives. As God created each of us with our own unique inventory of abilities, He had our function in mind. By discovering our design we uncover the mystery

In nothing has the church so lost her hold on reality as in her failure to understand and respect the secular vocation. She has allowed work and religion to become separate departments, and is astonished to find that, as a result, the secular work of the world is turned to purely selfish and destructive ends, and that the greater part of the world's intelligent workers have become irreligious, or at least, uninterested in religion. But is it so astonishing? How can anyone remain interested in a religion which seems to have no concern with nine-tenths of his life? The church's approach to an intelligent carpenter is usually confined to exhorting him not to be drunk and disorderly in his leisure hours, and to come to church on Sundays. What the church should be telling him is this: that the first demand that his religion makes on him is that he should make good tables.

—Dorothy Sayers
Creed or Chaos?

of our purpose.

> Every man's work, whether it be literature, or music, or pictures, or architecture, or anything else, is always a portrait of himself.
> —Samuel Butler

It's our job, then, to discover, submit, and develop those gifts. Only then will we find the competence to be the influence that God created us to be—no matter what level of influence He has in mind for us. When we do, the effects are dramatic. In *Finding a Job You Can Love,* Ralph Mattson and Arthur Miller write,

> When a man takes his correct position in creation, divine ecology falls into place and praise naturally emerges. Competence then manifests itself in work and play. . . .
>
> The incompetency we see everywhere is not because people lack gifts, but because they are not in the right place for their gifts. They are the stewards of what God has given them. There are plenty of gifts to do all the work that needs to be done everywhere and to do it gloriously well—so well, in fact, that people would go rejoicing from day to day over how much was accomplished and how well it was accomplished. But the world's systems, corrupted by the sin of man, place enormous obstacles in the way of each person who attempts to find his rightful place in creation. Such systems assume that people are fodder for their intentions.
>
> In short, most Christians as well as non-Christians do not understand what a job means and cannot address the world on the matter of widespread waste of human resources. Therefore they cannot make a redemptive difference. . . .
>
> The result is too many Christians performing incompetent, second-rate work, replacing

> For we are God's workmanship, created in Christ Jesus to do good works, which God prepared in advance for us to do.
> —Ephesians 2:10

the biblical command to redeem the time with an intention to "put in some time," an unsatisfactory result for the world and for the Kingdom.[3]

2. Accept the discipline of character.

Without character, the most gifted man or woman in the world will ultimately fail to influence anyone positively. God's goal for us as Christians is very clear—to conform us into the image of Christ. He achieves this goal in a number of ways, the most important of which is through intimacy with Christ Himself. Simply put, the more time I spend in intimate communication with Christ, the more He rubs off on me. Technically, more of Christ is coming to life in me. My old life is being exchanged for His new life. The more this balance shifts, the more like Christ I become.

Just as we have seen repeatedly in the life of Daniel, God also uses difficult circumstances to shape our character. Of particular importance in our present discussion is what God does with our gifts. In my experience, the very last thing most of us want to surrender to God is the use of our gifts. It is the most potent and personal thing about us. Willful person that I am, I want to be able to do my thing when I want to do it. Of all the evil things in me, this intent must die for me to be like Christ. The most devastating thing God can do to my old self is to put me in a position where I cannot use my gifts. There God reminds me, "These are My gifts. I can use them, or not use them, as I see fit."

> Genius is nothing but a greater aptitude for patience.
> —Benjamin Franklin

What that means to you is that at some time in your training and/or career, the thing that matters most to you—the practice of medicine—may be threatened or even actually taken away from you.

It will seem like your life is being put on hold and you will wonder where God is. He's actually right with you. He's just asking, "Are these My gifts? Are you going to let Me use them My way? Can you wait on My timing for Me to use them?"

I can honestly say that the misery of this kind of waiting is the most painful thing I have ever experienced. Yet God's reclaiming of His gifts is the most necessary part of my spiritual growth. Apart from it, I cannot be like Christ. Apart from Christ's control, my gifts can carry incredibly destructive potential. Only when they are in His hands and under His direction are they safe to use and able to accomplish His purposes.

3. Have the courage to swim in as big a pond as God places you in.

In our study of the Book of Daniel we have seen that a life following Jesus Christ fully is anything but a safe venture. It requires courage. You will meet opportunities and face obstacles that will challenge you to the edge of your faith. But remember, safety is in God's presence. Playing it safe is the most dangerous thing you can do if Jesus is leading you out of your comfort zone.

> It would be no surprise if a study of secret causes were undertaken to find that every golden era in human history precedes from the devotion and righteous passion of some single individual. This does not set aside the sovereignty of God. It simply indicates the instrument through which he uniformly works. There are no bona fide mass movements. It just looks that way. At the center of the column there's always one man who knows his God and knows where he is going.
> —Richard Ellsworth Day

Courage comes from a close walk with God. He is the only antidote to fear. The Lord told Joshua, "Have I not commanded you? Be strong and courageous. Do not be terrified; do not be discouraged, for the LORD your God will be with you wherever you go" (Joshua 1:9). When the heart is gripped by fear, the soul is frozen by inertia. When the heart is gripped by God, it is free to risk great things for Christ.

Courage also comes from absorbing the truth of God's Word. As Joshua led Israel into the land of Palestine, God told him, "Do not let this Book of the Law depart from your mouth; meditate on it day and night" (1:8).

There is a direct relationship between courage and the Scripture. God's Word fortifies us with the truth. It gives us the mental ammunition to do battle with the lies of Satan that would make us fall back in fear. Knowing that God is with us wherever we go will give us the courage to resist the fear and discouragement that Satan will doubtless throw in our path as we pursue God's will, the path of competence, character, and courage.

Courage comes from others. God is the One who gives courage, but sometimes we need to hear those words from someone else. That's what encouragement is all about. It's putting courage into someone else's heart. I can't count the times in men's small groups that someone has had just the right word or passage of Scripture that inspired courage in another person's battle. One person can make a difference, but not alone. More times

> Norman Vincent Peale found the impact of the Word in a little Swiss village near Lucerne. He writes, "Bergenstock is pervaded by the spirit of a remarkable man named Frederick Frey, who developed it. Born a peasant, Frey became an important figure in the Swiss power industry and then one of the greatest hotelkeepers in the world. His son Fritz once surprised me with the statement that his father's greatness arose out of a youthful sickness that required him to spend a year in the hospital. When I asked Fritz how that experience led to greatness, he said, 'During that year my father read the Bible six times.'
>
> "From that, Fritz said, his father developed such a faith that, if he were to walk a ridge with steep precipices on both sides, he would do it absolutely without fear: 'He was never afraid after the time he poured the Bible down inside himself.'"
>
> *—My Favorite Quotations*

than not, the one who has the courage to stand and change history has someone who encourages him or her when fear comes in to steal all sense of God's presence.

I don't know what God has put on your heart, but I will join Charles Cohn in challenging you: "Whatever it is, however impossible it seems, whatever the obstacle that stands between you and it, if it is noble, if it is consistent with God's kingdom, you hunger after it. You must stretch yourself to reach it." To do less would be tragic, for you, for medicine, and for our generation.

TIME FOR THOUGHT

DAY TWO: Use the following questions to stimulate your thought.

GROUP LEADER: Discuss these questions in the group after you have read the beginning text aloud together.

1. At the beginning of this chapter I said that it's easier to make a fortune than to make a difference. Do you agree? Why is one easier than the other? _____
   _____
   _____
   _____
   _____

2. What kind of influence is Christ having on your campus? Is it what you would like? _____
   _____
   _____
   _____
   _____

   How would you like things to change? _____
   _____
   _____
   _____

3. Have you ever thought of yourself as a person of destiny? Why or why not? _____
   _____

106

_____

_____

_____

4. Do you believe that one person can make a difference? Why? _____

_____

_____

_____

5. Why is influence superior to law or political power in bringing about change? _____

DAY THREE

_____

_____

_____

_____

Why have some Christians focused so heavily on political power in the eighties and nineties?

_____

_____

_____

_____

Has the kingdom of God really been furthered as a result? _____

_____

_____

6. What level of influence do doctors usually have? Why? _____

_____

_____

Do you know someone who has used his or her influence well? _____

_____

_____

_____

7. If you could influence anything or anyone, what would you love to see happen? _____

_____

_____

_____

_____

8. Why is competence important to Christ? To His kingdom? _____

_____

_____

_____

_____

_____

Do you see your studies as important to God?

_____

_____

_____

_____

_____

Why do you think Christians as a whole do not have a reputation of being the best students?

_____

_____

_____

_____

_____

9. What gifts do you think it takes to be a good doctor? _____

_____

_____

_____

_____

_____

_____

How can you hone the skills that medical school doesn't teach you? _____

_____

_____

_____

_____

_____

10. What character traits to you admire in the doctors you know? _____

_____

_____

_____

_____

_____

Have you ever known an arrogant doctor? Why are arrogance and Christian faith mutually exclusive? _____

_____

_____

_____

_____

How will you avoid becoming an arrogant doctor? _____

_____

_____

_____

_____

11. What motivated you to choose medicine as a career? _____

_____

_____

_____

12. How important is knowing your gifts to choosing the right residency? _____

_____
_____
_____
_____

13. Take a few moments and record the most important things you learned in this study. _____

_____
_____
_____
_____
_____
_____
_____
_____
_____
_____
_____

14. What important decisions did you make? ____

_____
_____
_____
_____
_____
_____
_____
_____
_____
_____
_____
_____

Notes

1. Robert Bezilla, ed., *Religion in America: 1990 Report* (Princeton, N.J.: The Princeton Religion Research Center, 1990), 60-61.
2. Charles Leerhsen, "Magic's Message," *Newsweek,* November 18, 1991, 59.
3. Ralph Mattson and Arthur Miller, *Finding a Job You Can Love* (Nashville, TN: Thomas Nelson Publishers, 1982), 41.

Christian Medical & Dental Associations

Changing Hearts in Healthcare

To order additional copies of this book or other resources
from CMDA's Life & Health Resources,
visit *www.shopcmda.org*
or call 888-230-2637

If you are interested learning more about CMDA's campus ministries or starting a student chapter,
visit *www.cmda.org/students*
or call 888-230-2637